Missionary
Carol
May God Bless You
Be Inspired
Bishop Carroll Johnson
24/10/2010

FAITH
Your Access Card
To The Kingdom of Heaven

Bishop Carroll R. Johnson, Jr.

FAITH—Your Access Card to the Kingdom of Heaven

PraiseWorkz Communications, Publishers
1928 Woodlawn Drive, Baltimore, MD 21207
www.maximumlifechurch.com

Printed in the United States of America
First Printing 2006

DEDICATED
TO

My Loving Wife, Pastor Muriel Johnson
and my Family, Elder Duane and Cynthia
and Nolan, Sherry and Tony Grant with
Chris, Drew & Jewel, and Keith. To My
parents, Elder Carroll & Delores Johnson,
Mother Mildred Willoughby, my Brothers
Alan & Michael and their families,
Sherman & Marvin Minor and their
families, all my relatives,
The Maximum Life Church Family, and
The Bible Way Church Family.
To our Lord and Savior Jesus Christ,
We Give You All The Glory!

Special Thanks to
Minister Angela Robinson
For Your Editing Help and Chapter Summaries

TABLE OF CONTENTS

FOREWORD

One of the least understood subjects presented in the Word of God is faith, and all of its implications. Yet faith is a most powerful gift that God has given to the human family. **Romans 12:3 says that "God gave to every man the measure of faith."**

"Faith Your Access Card to the Kingdom" is a very unique presentation of how most people are exercising faith without even realizing it. The tragedy is that people seem to find it easier to place their faith in that which has no sure foundation rather in the faithful, eternal God.

Bishop Carroll Johnson, Jr. has done a masterful job in demonstrating how faith is not wishful thinking, but ties into our ability to place our total confidence in the ability of God to work out His purposes for our lives when we invest in the divine storehouse.

I am confident that if this book is received with a mind to listen for the voice of the Spirit, it will result in consistent investments in the promises of God, and the kind of returns that accompany genuine faith.

To read this work is to discover many simple ways in which your potential can be released, simply by adhering to what heaven has already committed to you. To truly focus on reaching your full potential by virtue of what God has placed in you, I highly recommend this book for your library.

Bishop Alfred R. Reaves
Pastor
Church of the New Covenant

Chapter One
LORD, INCREASE OUR FAITH

"And the apostles said to the Lord, "Increase our faith." So the Lord said, "If you have faith as a mustard seed, you can say to this mulberry tree, 'Be pulled up by the roots and be planted in the sea,' and it would obey you."
Luke 17:5-6

As I write this book, I have been a Spirit filled Christian for thirty-six years and having been raised in the church my entire life, the word "faith" has been as familiar to me as breathing. I know about faith. I know the scriptures dealing with faith. As a full time Pastor with more vision than money in the bank, I exercise faith out of necessity every day. I have seen countless healing miracles as a result of faith in God and His Word. I have benefited by coming to salvation at a time when the "Word of Faith" teaching movement was blossoming and bombarding us with teaching on faith, healing, and prosperity. I have felt like I know about faith.

Recently, I have felt a sense that many of my loved ones, friends, colleagues, and members were under a Satanic attack in the area of their health. As my friend, Bishop Kola Onaolapa from Lagos, Nigeria was due to come to our church, the Lord led me to declare my wife's birthday, May 15, as Healing Sunday. Our objective was to preach and teach on faith and healing, and get every sick person we could to the service while we also would lift up those who were not able to physically be in attendance. There was a cry in my spirit that echoed that of the apostles in Luke 17:5, "Lord, Increase our faith." Over and over the Lord seemed to be saying to me, "Raise the Faith Level" and that has become a driving force and the motivation for this book and the current teaching.

As a young minister in 1976, I remember sitting at my desk as a manager at the Public Office of C&P Telephone and the Lord and I had a little conversation. He began to challenge me by simply stating that I did not know anything about "faith" and that it would be necessary for Him to begin a course of training for me in this subject. At first I was offended by His statement but He went on to explain that my entire life I had heard people talk about the Lord being a healer, but I had never been sick, nor had anyone in my immediate family circle been really sick. He said you have heard people talking about being "down to their last dime and the Lord stepping in right on time," but you've never missed a meal or seen your family's belongings on the sidewalk. Indeed, these words are no more real to you than just lyrics to songs. He reminded me that I had been educated at the best schools and had been recruited right into a nice paying job with great benefits. He emphasized to me that I really didn't know a thing about faith, but that he was sure going to teach me.

During that time my wife, Pastor Muriel, was pregnant with our youngest son, Keith and started having severe abdominal pain, particularly when getting in and out of the car. She was diagnosed with a grapefruit sized tumor that to remove would be a serious operation that could jeopardize her life as well as the baby. At the time I worked for the telephone company and had great health insurance so I sort of routinely made the arrangements for the operation and the blood bank. The Tuesday before the operation, I really began to think about all that was on the line for an operation of this magnitude in addition to the sight of me trying to cook (fast food was just really taking off back then), care for the house and two small kids while my wife was hospitalized and recuperating. Nothing associated with this situation was pretty and the Lord brought to my attention that in making all the arrangements, not once had I considered His ability to handle this problem.

It was actually startling to me that I had routinely listened to the doctor's prognosis and solution and just went headlong for it. I remembered the chorus to an old song we would sing, "Ask the Savior to help you," and realized that I hadn't even thought about asking God to perform the operation instead of the doctor. At my desk I "caught a hold of faith!" I called my wife and told her to get ready for our church's prayer meeting that night. We were going and God was going to heal her that night. It resonated with her and that evening she doubled over in pain as we went to church and as we arrived. At the end of the prayer time the dozen or so of us that were there at the Fellowship of the Jesus Associates that night gathered around Muriel and prayed for her healing. When we dismissed and got in the car, Muriel exclaimed, "THE PAIN IS GONE. I'M HEALED!" It was almost too much to believe, but as we drove the five minutes to our house our minds raced with the possibility. As she got out of the car, she again proclaimed that she had no more pain. A few minutes after we got home, Muriel let out a horrible scream from the bathroom. I went to investigate only to find that a bloody mass had passed out of her. We called my father and his calm reply was "the Lord is just getting rid of the tumor." We called the doctor and explained what happened and once she explained that she no longer had any pain, he made arrangements for her to be examined the next morning.

That day was one of the greatest days of our life as a team of doctors probed and questioned and Muriel kept explaining "you are not going to find anything because the saints prayed for me last night and God has healed me." After total bewilderment the doctor instructed his secretary to call the hospital and cancel the operation.

The Contagious Nature of Faith

Once my wife was healed it set off a healing wave that touched many people at our church and many people from other churches began coming to our Sunday evening services to experience healing. Faith, healing, and testimonies of blessings become contagious and people rightly start believing that if God can do it for one person, he is capable of doing it for me. As you read this book, it is my sincere prayer that God will increase your faith and that as you share your miracle that it will be a source of inspiration to others and that the fire of faith will move from "heart to heart and breast to breast."

As I reflect on how easily we accepted my wife's tumor and the doctor's solution without seeking a divine answer, I began to think about the number of troubling issues in our lives that we just have learned to live with and adjust to. We come to church Sunday after Sunday never looking for God to do anything about these issues and never expecting Him to solve them. We come for fellowship and a good time, to get a word of encouragement and go back to our routine. I am reminded of a passage in Luke 13:10 where the scripture records *"Now he was teaching in one of the synagogues on the Sabbath. And behold, there was a woman who had a spirit of infirmity eighteen years, and was bent over and could in no way raise herself up. But when Jesus saw her, He called her to Him and said to her, "Woman, thou are loosed from your infirmity." And He laid His hands on her, and immediately she was made straight, and glorified God."*

What strikes me about this story is that this woman had probably been coming to church routinely for eighteen years bent over and unable to raise herself up. Service after service, Sabbath after Sabbath, and even on this service with Jesus' reputation for healing, she was still not approaching Him for help. He didn't ask her if she wanted to be healed, but just out of compassion, he called to her, pronounced healing for her and laid His hands on her. To me this woman is a picture of most of the church each week except for those who have become absolutely desperate for divine intervention. Most of us have simply given in to our issues, adjusted our life and outlook to situations whether they be health, financial, relationships or vision related. As a result, we have lots of people praising God, dancing in the spirit, having a good time but we really don't need God for most of our exercises.

The truth is **you** have issues today in your life and in the lives of your loved ones and it is high time for us to come into the presence of the Lord with the full intention of appropriating the abundant life that Jesus promised to us through faith for every area of our lives. All over the church there are families struggling with issues of drug addiction, spousal abuse, failing marriages, sexual promiscuity, AIDS & HIV, disease, mental issues, homosexuality, bankruptcy, debt, and countless other problems that we will leave church still dealing with. Jesus spent over three years in the flesh demonstrating the power and potential available to us when we understand how to transact the business of our daily lives by depositing and withdrawing from the realm of the kingdom using our faith. Through faith we have access to the unlimited economy of heaven and I invite you to join me in a journey to investigate and appropriate the Banking System of the Kingdom of God!

Chapter One – Some Things to Think About

Just by picking up and reading this book, you have started the commitment to increase your faith. No matter how long you have served the Lord, your faith level must rest not only on hearing and believing His Word, but in truly trusting Him by your actions to supply every need in your lives.

Too often when we enjoy the blessings of God, we accept issues of life that He wants us to overcome if we can "catch hold of faith." As you begin the journey to investigate and enter into the Banking System of the Kingdom of God consider:

1. When was the last time you really depended on God and no one else – not even yourself – to do something supernatural for you?
2. Can you recall a moment in your life that God rescued you out of a desperate situation right in the nick of time?
3. What are the areas of your life that you need a divine answer to right now? (health? relationships? finances? vision?)

Chapter Two
Faith – The Currency of the Kingdom

"Now faith is the substance of things hoped for, the evidence of things not seen." Hebrews 11:1

Every sovereign nation or kingdom must have a convenient means for its citizens to buy and sell goods and services. Developed nations will have a formal banking system and their own currency authorized by the government and the banking system and it works because the citizens who accept the currency as payment have some degree of faith and confidence in it. In the United States of America we have a system of greenbacks with money printed by the government and administered by the Federal Reserve Bank. Other strong nations have their own currency such as the British Pound Sterling, the French Franc, the Canadian Dollar, and the Japanese Yen. Likewise, the Kingdom of God has its own currency: **our faith!** It is the required means of transacting business with God. If I go to Wal-Mart to buy a cartful of merchandise and attempt to pay for it with a stack of Japanese Yen, I will either be laughed out of the store or escorted to the security office or carted off to the "psych" ward of the nearest hospital. The currency that I offered was not pleasing to Wal-Mart and it did not satisfy their requirements for payment for the goods I wanted to acquire.

Hebrews 11:5 says that "without faith it is impossible to please Him." Jesus demonstrated over and over in His dealings with those in need of divine intervention for healing and miracles that "your faith has made thee whole." A quick example is the woman with the issue of blood in Matthew 9:20 which reads, *"And behold, a woman, which was diseased with an issue of blood twelve years, came behind him, and touched the hem of his garment: For she said within herself, If I may but touch his garment, I shall be whole. But Jesus turned him about, and when he saw her, he said, Daughter, thy faith hath made thee whole."* In other words, where natural or medically understood solutions were inadequate and people recognized that a supernatural kingdom solution was necessary, Jesus said that it could happen only as a result of the use of faith, the currency recognized for divine transactions.

In Hebrews 11:1, the word says that *"faith"* is the *"substance"* of the things we hope for. The Greek word for *"substance"* is *"hupostasis"* and it means that *"which stands under"* or the *"foundation"* or the *"basis."* If I stand on the raised pulpit of our church, I do so with the clear understanding that under the carpet there is a layer of plywood, and under the plywood there is framing lumber, and under the lumber there is a concrete slab, and under the slab there are several layers of stone, and under the stone there are layers upon layers of earth. Secondly, I would not have the courage to walk up on that pulpit if I did not have **faith** that it was **substantial** enough to hold my 245 pound body. My faith in the construction and substance of the pulpit gives me the courage to act in faith to take a position on the pulpit and use it for my purposes. Others did not even have the benefit of personally seeing the construction of the pulpit but will accept by faith that it will hold them and boldly walk up on it all the time. Likewise our faith in God and in the supernatural realm of the kingdom of God allows us to position ourselves in the purposes, abundance, healing and divine life of His kingdom with full confidence.

The Value of Your Substance

When we speak of something or someone having "*substance*" we mean there are facts and reality to back up the claims that relate to the person or thing. A person of *substance* has wealth. You may have many possessions and money, but the most important assets you have are primarily spiritual. Jesus put the value of our spiritual substance in context in Matthew 16:26 where He states *"For what profit is it to a man if he gains the whole world, and loses his own soul? Or what will a man give in exchange for his soul?"* The most valuable commodity you control is your ability to love and how you direct it or withhold it is the most powerful force at your disposal. Because God is love, His nature permeates the core of every person since we are all created in His image and likeness. The three most powerful words in the universe are "I Love You." There are multibillion dollar industries such as music, greeting cards, diamonds, flowers, weddings, etc. that are all built around the expression of our love for one another. The words have been carved on everything from tree trunks to bridges and buildings and it is so awesome that whatever our religious persuasion, educational background, social status or personality type, there is always someone who loves us, and someone that we love. Serial killers will still have Momma or a lover there at sentencing to stand up and say that their loved one is a good person. Love is a major component of your substance and an anchor of your faith portfolio.

Other important ingredients of your faith or substance portfolio are your energy, your creativity, your contacts, your time and your money. You may come up with other components, but when you understand the value of what you control and the impact that these have on your life and the world around you, you join with the Psalmist in proclaiming that we are *"fearfully and wonderfully made."* The most important decision you will make is how you choose to invest your faith or your substance and to which spiritual kingdom you will allocate your love, energy, creativity, contacts, time and money.

Faith as Our Title Deed

The Amplified Bible translates *"substance"* as *"title deed"* from its use in classical Greek as a real estate term signifying the document given at settlement as your proof of ownership of the property you have just purchased. In our economic system, a copy of the title deed is recorded in the public records of the city or county so that everyone can determine that you are the rightful owner of the property. Because you have the title deed to your property, you have the right to leave the settlement table and take the keys to the property, move your belongings in, decorate it to your taste, live in and enjoy the property. The deed **substantiates** or **faith's** that it is yours. You have a copy of the deed, the county has a copy of the deed, and your lender has a copy of the deed. In other words, you have an evidence of your ownership (faith), the county has an evidence of your lawful ownership (faith), and the lender has an evidence of your ownership (faith) and most likely requires that you occupy the property so they know you will take good care of it.

I would suggest that a similar system works in the Kingdom of God that allows you to appropriate things from God and your faith – title deed is held by you and recorded in your heavenly account as evidence to every spirit both angelic and demonic and every creature in the earth that what God has for you is for you. When God designed you he determined what he needed you to control and to operate with to fulfill His divine purpose through you. Every asset you need to perform his will has already been allocated to you, laid up for you, deeded to you, *faithed* to you, recorded for you and is waiting on you to experience the revelation of what has been assigned to your hands.

Paul writes in Ephesians 1:15, *"Therefore I also, after I heard of your faith in the Lord Jesus and your love for all the saints, do not cease to give thanks for you, making mention of you in my prayers: that the God of our Lord Jesus Christ, the Father of glory, may give to you the spirit of wisdom and revelation in the knowledge of Him, the eyes of your understanding being enlightened; that you may know the hope of His calling, what are the riches of the glory of His inheritance in the saints."*

Faith is the basis for every transaction in the kingdom. It is necessary to access the banking system of the Kingdom, to appropriate what has been assigned to us, it is your proof of ownership and gives you the confidence to occupy (do business and enjoy) the things that God has prepared for you. I urge you to go back and read this chapter again and take a few moments to meditate on what you have read!

Chapter Two - Some Things to Think About

All of us must transact business in our daily lives to survive and progress in our dreams and goals. It takes resources to transact business. Just like we conduct business on earth with our money, the Kingdom of Heaven has a currency that is the recognized means for conducting business—your faith!

Your faith carries more weight than anything you can see or touch because it is a "substance" that is guaranteed. This substance has more value than gold, land, or power because it is backed up, not by a banker, but by the God of the universe.

1. What are the ingredients or assets God has placed in your faith portfolio that He considers your "substance"?

2. Of all the elements in our faith portfolio, what is the most powerful?

3. Do you believe that when God fearfully and wonderfully made you, He deeded to you everything you would ever need to fulfill His plan for your life?

Chapter Three
The Whole World Operates By Faith

"For in Him we live, and move, and have our being."
Acts 17:28

Faith is inextricably tied to the spoken Word and since the Word is God, everything that has been created by His Word exists in an atmosphere of faith. We will elaborate later on the vital link between the spoken word and faith, but it is readily apparent from Genesis 1 that God not only decided what He would create, but every vision that He had for creation was activated by a *"and God said, let there be."* There is never any doubt that what He says will come to pass as He declares in Isaiah 55:10-11, *"For as the rain comes down, and the snow from heaven, And do not return there, But water the earth, And make it bring forth and bud, That it may give seed to the sower and bread to the eater, So shall my word be that goes forth from My mouth; It shall not return to me void, But it shall accomplish what I please, And it shall prosper in the thing for which I sent it."* This is the ultimate expression of confidence and faith that what God has spoken into existence will manifest and be sustained by His word. As a result, the earth keeps rotating, night and day keep occurring, the sun, moon, stars and galaxies keep doing what God said they would do. Plant, animal and human life keep reproducing just as he established and all mankind has come to accept by faith that all these systems and laws of nature and physics will operate as they have through observable history.

God has forced us into a world of faith because even with our advanced scientific and medical knowledge, we realize that we have only scratched the surface in actually understanding how most of the world and the human body operates. We are so fearfully and wonderfully made that most of the time we don't even give any thought to how oxygen gets distributed through our bodies and how our various body parts function unless something goes wrong. In order to be able to function in life without going crazy with anxiety about every facet of our life and surroundings all day, Paul states in Romans 12:3 *"that God has dealt to every man the measure of faith."* It is by faith a helpless baby comes into the world with the faith that if he or she can scream loud enough and long enough that someone will respond with food, a touch, or a dry diaper. The baby learns to have faith in the parents to provide everything it needs to thrive. As our life experiences broaden, our faith universe broadens with it.

It is amazing that in a world that prides itself on rational thinking and scientific knowledge, God has fixed life in such a way that the majority of our life transactions are "faith-based." From the time we are awakened by an alarm clock that we had faith would ring at the appointed time, we embark on a journey of faith that would scare us if we actually thought about it. We bath in water we feel confident is OK for bathing and most of us have enough faith in our municipal water systems that we will drink it at home and drink from water fountains practically anywhere in our city. We brush our teeth with toothpaste that we haven't the foggiest notion about its ingredients and we get into cars that we did not see manufactured and have faith that they will not konk out on us as we try to merge into 60 mile per hour highway traffic. We have faith that the other cars whizzing around us at 60 and 70 miles per hour will remain in their lanes even while the drivers are talking on cell phones, applying makeup and these days even watching movies as they drive. We purchase food from grocery stores and take it home and eat it even though we don't have any idea where the food came from. We eat food from restaurants that has been prepared by people that we never even see in conditions that we don't even wonder about. We go to jobs and work hard for weeks by faith that we will receive a paycheck in the amount we were promised. We will even have faith that they will directly deposit our pay in our account at our bank that by faith we believe will still be in business when we get there and still have our funds available.

When we first started our church in Randallstown, **Old Court Savings and Loan** had their headquarters a few blocks from our church at Liberty and Old Court Roads. As we drove past the bank one day, we noticed a line of people at the door. Later, one of our members called to say that there were rumors of problems at the bank and if we had any money in there, we should immediately join the line and withdraw our funds. He was right because shortly after that, the bank closed and everyone that didn't get in there in time lost all their money and found out that the bank was only insured by the State of Maryland and in the ensuing savings and loan scandals, thousands of people lost their hard earned money.

Speaking of our money, it is interesting that at one time in this country, our banking system operated on a "gold standard." In other words, our paper money was based on gold bricks supposedly in Ft. Knox. Well, it's been many years since there was anything like that backing our currency. Our money is backed up by the "**full faith** and credit of the United States Government." Since we are the government then our money is backed only by our faith in each other and this idea we call the United States of America.

It doesn't matter how educated you are, how atheistic or agnostic you are, how secular humanist you are, God has set this planet up in such a way that nearly everything you do every day requires the exercise of faith. By faith you select a marriage partner knowing full well that you just don't really know if it's going to work out. You know the statistics are not favorable for your marriage lasting, but by faith you spend thousands on the wedding, the honeymoon, and setting up house. When you part ways in the morning it is by faith that you pray that your spouse will remain or has been faithful in your relationship. You just don't know for sure. By faith you send your children off to school, but you really don't know if they've been going faithfully or making a real effort after they get there. By faith you believe your children are not experimenting or hooked on drugs. By faith, you believe that your children are not engaged in sexual activities. By faith you hope your Pastor is not committing adultery or is a closet homosexual or is stealing all the funds. By faith you believe that your company's pension plan will actually have money in it for you when you retire. By faith, millions will get on airplanes today and have faith that the pilots, the planes, and the air traffic control system will get you and your luggage to your destination.

God has forced us all into lives of incredible faith! Those of us who believe that God has written a script for our lives must ponder that the Hebrew writer describes Jesus in Hebrews 12:2 as *"the author and finisher of our faith."* He is the author of all the stories of our life that are designed to bring us to a perfect state and use of faith.

Unconscious vs. Conscious Faith

The nervous system of the body is one of the most

complex wonders of the universe. It consists of two primary systems, the Central Nervous System (CNS) and the Peripheral Nervous System (PNS). The Central Nervous System consists primarily of our brain and spine and the Peripheral Nervous System is the system outside of CNS that services our limbs and organs. The PNS is further broken down into the Somatic Nervous System (SMS) and the Autonomic Nervous System (ANS). Hang in here for a moment! The CNS affects our conscious mental activity where our ANS regulates the organs of our body such as our heart, stomach, and intestines. In most situations we are unaware of the workings of the ANS because it functions in an involuntary, reflexive manner. We don't have to use our minds to think about regulating our heart rate or the secretion of chemicals in our stomach to digest our food because the ANS takes our mind off this stuff. Thank God for that!

So much of our lives require us to accept things by faith that the measure of faith given to us operates mostly on an unthinking, unconscious level. So most of the time we will just walk on the floors of our house without wondering whether they will cave in and we'll drive under countless bridges in a day without fear that they will drop on us. Now we are well aware that sometimes roads just open up gigantic holes, and we know that bridges collapse, and tires go flat, and axles break, and sometimes those big trucks on the other side of the line come across on the wrong side. It's as if God has built into us an Autonomic Faith System (AFS) to be able to get through life without losing our minds with fear.

On the other hand, our quality of life is greatly impacted by our Central Nervous System (CNS) and what we do with the information gathered by our senses. How we react to our senses and act on the thoughts of our mind becomes the focal point for our conscious enjoyment of life. We derive pleasure from making plans and carrying them out and each time we complete one of these simple cycles of life, we have used our faith in a conscious way. We visualize what we will wear and eat, and where we will go and what we will say, and each day is really a triumph of the faith that we have that we can actually fulfill what we visualized. In a normal healthy person, we certainly don't give enough thought or thanks for how well our PNS and our organs are working until we start having some health issues, but the fact is that most of our waking hours are consumed with what we are cooking up in our brains.

God is interested in us pursuing a conscious development of our faith and having a clarity about where we direct our faith and how we use our faith. We must study faith and examine ourselves to see whether we are in the Faith and develop our faith senses and lift the level of what we visualize to ever higher levels to conform to the Lord's vision for our lives.

Life Can Put a Hurt on Our Faith

Faith— Access Card To The Kingdom of Heaven

As we live, we get the opportunity to interact with people and things that we routinely put our faith in from our parents, to our cars, to our employers, to our love interests, to our religious leaders and churches, and even to our politicians and government. The longer we live the more opportunities we have to experience disappointment and devastation from people and systems that betray our faith. We also have more and more opportunities to see things not seem to work out the way we had visualized them. These seeming failures or disappointments can take a toll on your faith.

Boy, do I remember the trauma of my sixth-grade romance with Debbie B. The kids in my class came up with a great way to advance relationships by going to the Walbrook Movie Theater where the darkness provided a great cover to kiss (that's as much as we envisioned in the sixth-grade in those days). The only problem was they chose to go on Sunday's and I had to go to church, so since I wasn't available, my classmate Victor was able to step in. When I got to school on that Monday, I was devastated to learn that I had been jilted by my sixth-grade girl. I'm sure you have your own story of your first taste of betrayal of faith that makes one a little more cautious the next time around. Cars let us down, friends and parents let us down, jobs give us pink slips, politicians lie to us, often times churches and leaders break our hearts. People who went through the Depression sometimes hide their money under the mattress rather than put their faith in the bank or a broker. Millions of married couples are left in tattered ruin after learning that their spouse has been unfaithful and often have a difficult time putting their faith in anyone again. It seems that the longer we live the more skeptical and cynical we become to people, things and institutions.

When Jesus was teaching about the signs of the end of the age, He says in Matthew 24:12 *"And because lawlessness will abound, the love of many will grow cold."* Because people experience so much unfaithfulness, our society increasingly suffers from a lack of commitment in every area of our life. As a result people decide to "shack up" rather than commit to marriage, divorce as quickly as the seasons change, and switch churches with every passing fad or correction. There is so much to destroy our faith, that Jesus asks the question in Luke 18:8 *"...Nevertheless, when the Son of Man comes, will He really find faith on the earth?"* The vital answer lies in where we direct our substance and who becomes the primary object of our faith. The Psalmist says in 118:8-9 *"It is better to trust in the Lord Than to put confidence in man. It is better to trust in the Lord Than to put confidence in princes."*

We can safely put our faith and direct our substance to the purposes of God in full confidence that *"He is a rewarder of them that diligently seek Him." Hebrews 11:6* If you have been devastated and left confused about the use of your faith in relationships and even in the things of God, I encourage you to get back in the flow of life. God has determined that you must live by faith. Without the conscious application of faith, you really are not living. Dream again, love again, become passionate again. As Rev. Jesse Jackson would say, "keep hope alive!"

Chapter Three - Some Things to Think About

God has designed a world that forces us to place faith in systems and laws of nature and physics with every breath we take.   Eventually we even forget to take thought of the gravity that keeps us on the ground, the heart that keeps ticking, and the fact that we wake up every morning.

But as life throws calamities our way, we slowly begin to lose faith. Our experiences in things or people that fail, teach us to doubt. We begin to trust half of what we see and none of what we hear. In the faith-based atmosphere God created, He intends not for us to be discouraged, but to learn to develop and direct our faith to higher levels to fulfill the purposes of God.

1. Are there areas in your life that disappointment and pressure have caused you to unconsciously face with fear and doubt?

2. Is the level of your faith in your relationships, your job, your finances, your strength, based on your experiences or on confidence in God?

3. What percent of the time do you trust your family to do what they say? What percent do

you depend on your job to supply your need? Do you trust God to be God 100% of the time?

Chapter Four
Understanding Your Faith Accounts

"...God has dealt to each one a measure of faith."
Romans 12:3

Since God has started each of us with a measure of faith, I am using this starting faith balance as akin to an initial deposit in our heavenly faith account. In the banking system of the kingdom then we have a personal account established in our name that allows us to complete transactions related to our life and purpose in God's economy. We have talked about the necessity of using our faith assets nearly all day every day just to carry on our normal daily activities. We are constantly making faith deposits and withdrawals in our various faith accounts. Before we accept salvation in Jesus Christ, we operate in a fog of faith ignorance, not understanding that the grace of God has given us a measure of faith and that God *"makes His sun rise on the evil and on the good, and sends rain on the just and the unjust." Matthew 5:45.* It is a grace or trust account that he has opened for all men so that they can operate in a faith-based world.

In the Garden of Eden, Adam and Eve voluntarily placed their faith and assets in the hands of Satan by hearing and following his words. God had given them access to all the resources of Eden and the whole earth if they just heeded the words they had heard from him and continued to exercise faith in the validity of what they had heard. They had an unlimited portfolio of kingdom faith accounts and assets that they blew by misplacing their faith. They got evicted from their Garden of Eden estate, lost access to the tree of life and all the other life sustaining assets of the Garden, and were left with just the measure of faith that would allow them to live in the world for a rapidly declining set of years. Their remaining assets had been voluntarily placed under the control of Satan whose words they had placed their faith in.

Water Baptism

In salvation, a wonderful transaction takes place with regard to our kingdom accounts and assets. When we come to accept the Word of God and His promises to us, we do so with a public act of confessing with our mouth the Lord Jesus and believing in our hearts that God raised Him from the dead as His Word teaches and we shall be saved. (Romans 10) We publicly acknowledge our faith in him through water baptism. It is interesting that the

Greek word *"baptizo"* was used in classical Greek as a banking term meaning "to be placed in someone's account." When we are baptized we are publicly announcing that we are voluntarily removing our accounts from Satan's control to be deposited into the personal account of Jesus Christ. Our life and assets are being immersed and merged in His life and assets. The shedding of His precious blood on Calvary has purchased our account and redeemed us from the cursed account management of the devil, who used us and our assets for his own evil purposes. Our assets have been under the control of a murderer and a thief who had no other plans but to steal from us, to kill us and to destroy us, but thank God Jesus has *"come that we might have life and that more abundantly!" (John 10:10)*

The Condition of What You Bring

When you make a deposit in your bank account, the bank really doesn't make a big deal over the form or condition of what you bring. You can bring cash or coin of just about any condition. You can bring checks or money orders and again they can be of just about any amount or condition. Likewise, the Lord will take us for deposit no matter what condition we may be in. He doesn't care about our age, size, educational background, race, gender, health, the sins of our past, our quirks or anything else that people judge us by. No matter what has happened in our past, our Lord knows exactly what he originally designed us for and what lies dormant within us and exactly how He plans to bring our potential to the surface.

The bank doesn't ask where the funds came from or how you obtained them, but the teller simply accepts what you have and deposits the funds in your designated account. The checks may have the name of another individual or company on them, but once you endorse the check it becomes identified with you and loses its former identity as it becomes one with your other assets in that account.

At the time you come to Jesus Christ to be deposited in His designated account for you, you are the product of a lot of input from many sources and experiences. No matter what degree of success we may have achieved in our eyes or the opinions of others, we are reminded that in the face of God's perfection all our righteousness is as filthy rags. We don't have enough to qualify on our own to be identified with him. From time to time, I receive offers from investment brokerage firms that would like to handle my account. Some are targeted to high net worth individuals (they got my name from somewhere – you know the saying, "fake it 'til you make it") that require a minimum investment of $25,000. Most of the time I haven't had enough funds to qualify. I am so grateful that it is not our assets or goodness that allows us to be deposited and identified with the Lord but His blood has made us worthy and to be counted as one with Him.

Baptism of The Holy Spirit

Water baptism is our public deposit into the account of Jesus Christ to become an asset of His to be used for His purposes as He sees fit. It is us becoming identified with Him by an act of our will. In the baptism of the Holy Spirit, the Lord turns the tables and by an act of His will, He deposits himself in us. In John 14:23, Jesus said, *"If anyone loves Me, he will keep My word; and My Father will love him, and We will come to him and make Our home with him."* Can you believe the increased value of flawed human beings who suddenly become earthen vessels where the very Spirit of God takes up residence. Jesus assured His disciples that not only was He coming but the Father would also be moving in and depositing Himself in those who keep His words. In Acts 1:8 our Lord's last words to his disciples were that they would *"receive power when the Holy Spirit has come upon you, and you shall be witnesses to Me in Jerusalem, and in all Judea Samaria, and to the end of the earth."* It is an unbelievable transaction that we would be selected to have this treasure be in our earthen vessels and that saints would be recipients of the revelation that makes *"known the riches of the glory of this mystery among the Gentiles: which is Christ in you, the hope of glory." Colossians 1:27*

The smartest investment you could ever make is to be baptized in the Name of Jesus (deposit your life and your assets in His account), because it triggers a reciprocal deposit of Christ in you. There is no other transaction in the universe that can enhance your value to such a magnitude. It brings you into the royal family and makes you a joint-heir with Jesus Christ. By placing your life and your faith into the account of Jesus Christ and allowing your assets to be under His control you become His peculiar treasure, kept by the power of God and a tool for blessing all the families of the earth. You see when funds are deposited in an account, they don't just sit idle like possessions placed in a safe deposit box. Instead, they are designated for circulation under management of savvy investors to improve the lives of others and the community.

In Genesis 12 God lays out to Abraham the benefits He planned for him if he was willing to accept His faith assignment. It reads, *"Now the Lord had said to Abram: "Get out of your country, From your family And from your father's house, To a land that I will show you. I will make you a great nation; I will bless you And make your name great; And you shall be a blessing, I will bless those who bless you, And I will curse him who curses you; And in you all the families of the earth shall be blessed."* In other words He was saying to Abraham that at this stage of your life you have achieved a certain value, but if you will take me up on my offer and convert your energy to following my investment plan for you, you will greatly increase the value of your life. The very simple fact of life is that placing your life in God's hands and seeking to know and cooperate with His designs for us increases the value of our life in ways that are exceedingly, abundantly above anything that we can ask or think.

Jesus describes the Holy Spirit as the "Helper" in the New King James or the "Comforter" in the King James Version. The word means "one called in alongside, or an advocate, attorney, or counselor." The Holy Spirit is an expert on the Laws of the Kingdom since he wrote them so we couldn't have a better attorney representing us and giving us legal counsel. But the Holy Spirit is also aware of our purpose and what resources have been assigned to us and is able to take our feeble understanding of the plans and translate them into a proper request at the Bank of the Kingdom of God!

We have an attorney with access to the bank vault. It makes a lot of sense to be sure you have been filled with the Spirit and keep being filled and do all you can to spend as much of your time in the presence of the Lord. He has promised to lead you and to guide you into all truth and Paul says in I Corinthians 2:12 *"Now we have received, not the spirit of the world, but the Spirit who is from God, that we might know the things that have been freely given to us by God."*

Chapter Four - Some Things to Think About

In the banking system of heaven, God has a faith

account with only your name on it that you can deposit into and withdraw from in this earthly realm. Whatever you deposit is instantly redeemed by removing control from Satan and putting it under the control of Jesus Christ.

The first and most important asset you can deposit into the account of Jesus is yourself! God never judges the condition of the deposit, only the sincerity of the depositor. As you deposit with him, he is faithful to return your investment in countless ways you can only imagine.

1. What is the most valuable thing you feel you possess?

2. Do you feel you have control over your life and the things God has entrusted to you?

3. What actions can a person take to deposit himself into the Kingdom of God?

4. Do you have "assets" that you have reserved for your use that you would now be willing to deposit with God?

Chapter Five
Converting Your Assets To The Realm of Faith

*"Honor the Lord with your possessions, And with the
first fruits of all your increase;
So your barns will be filled with plenty, and your vats
will overflow with new wine."*
Proverbs 3:9-10

Currency Conversions

Every sovereign nation has its own currency and
if you are content to stay within the confines of
your own country, you will have little interest in how
the value of your currency stacks up against other
currencies. If you are a US citizen and never have
to travel abroad or do business with international
contacts, you won't really care about the British
Pound Sterling. However, if you are going to visit

London or move there to spend some time, you will immediately be impacted regarding the value of the US Dollar versus the British Pound. I remember going to London recently and as we were about to leave BWI Airport here in Baltimore, I stopped at the currency exchange to convert some dollars to pounds. I gave them $100 and they gave me $55 back in pounds. It was an awful feeling to begin a trip knowing that every one of my dollars would only be worth half in its value in London. So, everyday traders establish the value of your currency against that of other nation's currencies.

Listed below are some examples of what $100 US would convert to in other nations as of June, 2005:

$100 US = 55 British Pound Sterling
$100 US = 125 Canadian
$100 US = 246 Brazil
$100 US = 673 South Africa
$100 US = 827 China

Therefore, if you were able to do business in South Africa or China, you can see that your money could buy a lot more goods or services there as opposed to even in the US. We call this a favorable exchange rate. On the other hand, to do business in London would have a negative impact because of an unfavorable exchange rate.

Because we have been born again from above, we have the privilege of operating in two realms. We have been legally adopted into the Kingdom of Our

Lord and Savior Jesus Christ. We are members of His royal family and according to Philippians 3:20 *"our citizenship is in heaven"* (New King James Version). Since "faith" is the currency of the kingdom of heaven, it is then necessary for us to learn how to convert our earthly assets into 'faith-based' assets or currency so that we can do business in the kingdom realm. The exciting thing is that the exchange rate between earthly and heavenly is decidedly favorable for you.

Throughout the Bible there are countless examples of what happens when we present earthly stuff for spiritual. When you go to the currency exchange counter, you offer them the currency of your current nation to obtain the currency of the other nation. As we boldly approach the throne of grace to obtain mercy and find grace to help in times of need, we offer to God our assets such as our will, our time, our creativity, our praise and worship, our goods and our money, and it converts according to our faith. The exchange rate is flexible so that it is able to meet whatever the need is, regardless of its comparison to what we have offered or what is in our faith account.

The Faith Card

As I was preparing this book, I was thinking about the currency exchange issues in going to London. After, my initial trade at the Currency Exchange at BWI, I told my wife that rather than be bothered with trying to deal with learning the British currency and carrying a lot of it around, we would just use our Visa Bank Card for everything we possibly could. You know the slogan *"Visa, It's Everywhere You Want to Be."* It really worked out well because every purchase whether the subway, restaurants, clothing, theater, ice cream – it was simple, we just used the access card. Whether it was a small purchase or something that cost hundreds, the bank card worked. I didn't have to be constantly confronted with the bitter taste of the exchange rate and I was confident that there was enough money available on the card to meet every need on the trip.

I designed a Faith Access Card styled like a credit card to use as a bookmark and promotional companion to this book. It's a bookmark particularly for your Bible that serves as a constant reminder that when we use our faith we can appropriate all that God has for us and that we have an unlimited balance available to us. Even though we have invested substance in our kingdom accounts, our available balance is whatever is needed for our assignment.

In one of his books Watchman Nee talks about the municipal water system where he describes the reservoir and a series of pipes that bring the water through the city and to each house. The pipes that leave the reservoir are very large to enable them to carry enough water capacity and pressure to service the city. As pipes branch off the water mains, they are smaller and smaller until they reach the house. The beauty is that the supply and the pressure are enough to fill up any size pipe that is connected. If you have bigger pipes, you will have the ability to have more water and more water pressure (power). God's power is sufficient to handle any size dream, no matter how big or how small. The limiting factor is not the supply, but the capacity of our pipes. Enlarge your vision and God's power is more than sufficient to supply all your needs!

The Conversion Miracle of the Loaves and Fish

In one of the most celebrated miracles of Jesus in John chapter 6, a large crowd of between 5,000 to 15,000 people have been diligently following Him and soaking up His teaching. When Jesus notes that the people are tired and hungry, He instructs the disciples to feed them. They are perplexed about several things regarding this directive.

First, even though they seem to have enough money in the treasury to purchase food for everyone, there does not seem to be enough supply available in the local towns. Secondly, the disciples seem to feel uncomfortable with spending that amount on these people, and encourage Jesus to send them away and let them fend for themselves.

He then begins one of the most dramatic lessons on conversion that the world has ever witnessed. They find a boy with a lunch of five barley loaves and two small fish, and Jesus decides that would be a perfect offering for conversion. The lad was willing to offer his lunch obviously having the faith that he would not go hungry. Jesus lifted up the offering and gave thanks and began to distribute parts to the disciples who in turn broke their parts up and began distributing to the people. The Bible says that the whole multitude enjoyed an all-you-can-eat meal and they wound up with 12 baskets of leftovers. Each of the apostles got to take home a "saint's bag" as a reminder of how favorable the exchange rate with heaven is.

In Luke 17:5-6, the apostles said to the Lord, *"Increase our faith." "So the Lord said, "If you have faith as a mustard seed, you can say to this mulberry tree, 'Be pulled up by the roots and be planted in the sea,' and it would obey you."* The exchange rate is unlimited. It's whatever you need for the situation. There is no proportional exchange like the earthly currency converters. Jesus is saying that if the job requires mulberry trees flying off into the sea, mustard seed sized faith is OK.

The exchange factor can be logarithmic as in Joshua 23:10 where the scripture reads *"One man of you shall chase a thousand,"* and Leviticus 26:8 says, *"Five of you shall chase a hundred and a hundred of you shall put ten thousand to flight."* The Bible is full of examples of great victories from small numbers of people such as David against Goliath, Gideon's 300 against a host of Midianites and Amalekites that were as numerous as locusts and whose camels were without number, and King Jehoshaphat's praise singers leading the army of Israel to victory over the armies of Moab, Ammon, and Mt. Seir.

We have the assurance that no matter who or what is stacked against us that *"greater is He that is in us than he who is in the world,"* and as Elisha assured his servant in 2 Kings 6:16 when it appeared that the Syrian army had surrounded them *"Do not fear, for those who are with us are more than those who are with them."*

Put Your Time In

There is a time conversion laid out in Psalms 84:10 where the scripture reads *"For a day in Your courts is better than a thousand. I would rather be a doorkeeper in the house of my God than dwell in the tents of wickedness."* In other words, David had calculated from his experience that spending one day in the house of the Lord was equivalent to 1,000 days spent anywhere else. Most of us don't spend an entire 24 hour period in church at a time, but let's take a 4 hour period that we might devote to God's house with Sunday School, Worship service and maybe some time in choir rehearsal.

Using David's exchange rate for his time,

1 Day in church = 1,000 days anywhere else
4 Hours in church = 166 days anywhere else

There is an old adage that time is money and you may work in a job with a clear hourly rate. Let's take a nice salary of $20 an hour, so in your normal time exchange you get paid $160 for an 8 hour day or

$80 for 4 hours. This would amount to a little over $41,000 per year. Using our church exchange rate above, we get a value of:

4 Hours in church = 166 days anywhere else @ $80 per day = $13,280

So then every Sunday I devote to church would be like depositing $13,280 in my kingdom faith account. If I devote 4 hours in church a week for 52 weeks in a year, my time in church by David's exchange equals $690,560 per year. Check it out:

4 Hours in church = $13,280 each week x 52 weeks in a year = $690,560 per year

If you were offered a job that required 4 hours per week to make $690,560 per year, would you take it over a job that required you to work 40 hours and make $41,000. David said he would take the janitor's job in church rather than a job anywhere else. Any person with a mustard seed sized brain would see this deal and show up for church every time the door was open. Friend, for this kind of exchange you should beg for a church key and find every excuse you can to let your feet strike Zion. This is not rocket science if you believe the Bible to be the Word of God and you have faith in what it says.

Look again at how David starts out this Psalm 84.

"How lovely is your tabernacle, O Lord of hosts!

My soul longs, yes, even faints for the courts of the Lord; My heart and my flesh cry out for the living God. Even the sparrow has found a home, and the swallow a nest for herself, Where she may lay her young - Even your altars, O Lord of hosts, My King and my God. Blessed are those who dwell in Your house; They will still be praising you. Selah."

Jesus and The Rich Young Ruler

Jesus understood how difficult it is for people to see the wisdom of exchanging earthly assets for kingdom faith currency. That's why he spent so much time teaching and using examples dealing with money. In Luke 18:18-30 there is the story of the rich, young ruler who approached Jesus with how to inherit eternal life. After a discussion about his religious habits, Jesus challenged him to take a faith step and convert his earthly assets into faith currency by selling everything that he owned, distributing it to the poor and thereby converting it into faith currency in heaven.

Verse 22 states *"So when Jesus heard these things, He said to him, "You still lack one thing. Sell all that you have and distribute to the poor, and you will have treasure in heaven; and come, follow me."* Ouch, crunch time! This is where the rubber meets the road for all of us when it comes to believing that the conversion or offering of our stuff and time for kingdom purposes is worth more than our devotion to our stuff and the acquisition of it. Is it worth more in our hands than in His? Are we more enhanced by following our agenda than His?

Obviously as Jesus and the apostles watched this young man choose to hold on to his possessions and give up on the opportunity for eternal life and actually hanging out everyday with the Creator of the Universe in a human body, they had some questions. Peter said, "See, we have left all and followed you." These guys had put their businesses and family life on hold and although they were having all their needs met, they had some questions about the long-term program. Jesus' response is one of the clearest statements in scripture on the benefits of kingdom currency conversion, *"So He said to them, "Assuredly, I say to you, there is no one who has left house or parents or brothers or wife or children, for the sake of the kingdom of God, who shall not receive many times more in this present time, and in the age to come eternal life."* Matthew's account of this incident in chapter 19:29 says that you will receive *"a hundredfold"* return in this life. In other words, convert everything you offer to God at the rate of **one hundred fold.**

We used to have a song that said "It pays to serve Jesus, It pays everyday, It pays every step of the way."

The Far Reaching Effects of Converted Assets

Earlier we talked about the conversion of the little boy's lunch to the realm of the spirit and as a result thousands of people were able to eat that day. The effect of sowing natural stuff for kingdom purposes is mind-blowing. When my brothers and I were growing up, my father would often play the organ at church for Praise Service and on Friday nights for Bishop Winfield Showell's Bible Study.

My brothers Alan and Michael Sandy and I were fascinated by the organ and piano and we would beg our parents to take us back to church on Sunday evenings when the Echoneers choir would sing. They always had great musicians and we would sit behind them and just watch them play as we imagined ourselves playing. My father has never been into materialism and growing up on the edge of the Depression tended to make him not interested in spending money on stuff. But, every once in a while, he would come through in a shocking way. When I was in the seventh grade, I got home from school and to our astonishment, a delivery truck pulled up with a Hammond organ. Our lives changed so drastically and permanently that day, because we were so excited about learning to play that Mom and Dad had to pretty much create a schedule so that we wouldn't fight over whose turn it was to play. Our parents took time to teach us what they knew, and Elder Johnny Coates (now Bishop) would come over every week and teach us what he knew and we were changed for the rest of our lives.

When the first organ wasn't quite as sophisticated as we needed, we came home another day and Dad had gotten us a more expensive model. We've been blessed to be musicians in the house of the Lord, but probably millions have been touched by the gift of music that was unleashed through us over the past 40 years. That organ came at a time when the guys in my neighborhood were just beginning to experiment with crime and sex with several of my close buddies beginning to go to jail and father children by the 9th and 10th grade.

I began investing all my love, energy, creativity, contacts, time and money in playing the organ so that I really didn't have the time or the interest to hang out with them anymore. I chose to go to a different high school than most of them and that moved me further away from their antics. Who knows what the investment in that organ saved us from! The conversion of $1,000 cash to spiritual purposes yielded a return of 3 saved young men who have dedicated their lives to bringing people into the presence of the Lord.

Out of this passion for music I became interested in recording and producing albums and eventually this led to the founding of Praise Recordings along with support from my pastor, now Bishop Alfred Reaves and Al Stewart and others. It eventually became Baltimore's first Black owned 16-Track recording studio and led to Zamar Music Group which released music around the world in partnership with Dr. Leonard Scott of Tyscot Records and Benson Music.

Promise to Our Seed

We talked about how water baptism places our assets in the account named Jesus and puts us in the position to receive the reciprocal deposit of His Spirit in us through the Baptism of the Holy Spirit. In Peter's great sermon on the Day of Pentecost he first quotes Joel's prophecy *"And it shall come to pass in the last days, says God, that I will pour out of My Spirit on all flesh; Your sons and your daughters shall prophesy, Your young men shall see visions,..."* *Acts 2:17*, and later in the sermon he states *"For the promise is to you and to your children, and to all who are afar off, as many as the Lord our God will call."* *Acts 2:39.*

My wife and I have been blessed to raise three brilliant children in Elder Duane Johnson, Sherry Grant, and Keith Johnson and we now have 4 exceptional grandchildren, Chris, Drew, Jewel and Nolan. The gifts of music, creativity, and technology are in their DNA and from their birth they have been immersed in the creative arts. Duane has ministered to millions as one of the nation's top radio personalities both on WEAA at Morgan State University and Baltimore's premier station 92Q.

Sherry has been blessed to be a prolific Playwright and become the founder of the Showtime Theatre (www.newshowtimetheatre.com) to produce cutting-edge kingdom theater. Her first play, "Preacher's Kids, The Good, Bad, & the Ugly," debuted at the Baltimore Arena in June, 2000 to an audience of nearly 7,000 and featured Beyonce Knowles and

Destiny's Child. The play later went on the road with members of the Winan's family.

Keith is the music genius who co-founded the Showtime Theatre with Sherry and serves as the musical director but has as his primary focus the development of a cable TV network for musicians as well as an internet 24 Hour TV Channel for the kingdom called www.worshipnetworktv.com.

We are being amazed every day as we see the generation of the grandchildren beginning to do great exploits as 13 year old Chris shoots the video for the church TV show, and nine year old Drew created "The Joke of the Day" for his school where each morning he goes on his school's internal TV system and starts the day off with the medicine of laughter. Even the babies Jewel and Nolan are clearly into microphones and performing.

My father's investment in that organ even reaches beyond our immediate family because when the recording studio became my full-time occupation, my aunt Doris asked me to come take my younger cousin Craig with me to work. That little guy fell in love with the cables and the sound business and is now a nationally known sound engineer and consultant doing PA and sound installs in churches everywhere as the President of his own company, Collins Audio.

Who knows how many lives will eventually be

touched by the conversion of that $1,000 to kingdom investment.

Chapter Five - Some Things to Think About

As we operate with our faith currency in the earth an amazing exchange is going on in the spirit realm. Whatever we invest in the natural into the kingdom is able to be converted to meet the specific need and is able to increase to meet the entire shortfall! Everything we bring to God's kingdom can be instantly recognized and utilized.

The measure of our faith is the only limit to the return in the kingdom of God. All that God desires for us is available. But it comes in response to the size of our vision and our needs. God has the unlimited capacity to give us as great a victory as we are willing to believe.

1. Can you think of an investment you made with God that produced a hundredfold return?

2. In God's arithmetic, how many days are worth one day in the court's of the Lord? What would the value of such a day be in man's terms?

3. Does the success of faith in God depend of the quantity of what we put into the situation?

4. Before you "exchange" your substance with God, do you try to reason out the value you will get in return?

Chapter Six
Becoming Comfortable In the Kingdom Of God

"For we walk by faith, not by sight." II Corinthians 5:7

When Adam was created God made him in His image and likeness and planted him in the earth environment that had been enveloped in darkness and chaos as a result of Lucifer being cast out of heaven and into this realm with a host of fallen angels. Lucifer or Satan is called the Prince of the Power of the Air meaning he represents a spiritual kingdom (vertical) that inhabits or "sits down" in the midst of the earth realm and attempts to exert influence in the culture and affairs of the inhabitants of earth. As God began speaking light and life into the earth environment, man was created as a divinely influenced and connected invasion force to *"Be fruitful and multiply; fill the earth and subdue*

51

it.." Genesis 1:28. They were to operate within the gravity based earth realm (horizontal kingdom), with a constant connection with God (vertical kingdom). The scripture records that God and Adam met and talked every day as God mentored him in even naming everything in his realm, so that Adam became adept at operating in the earth realm while at the same time being so comfortable in dealing with God in the spirit realm that he didn't even realize that he was naked. Since faith comes by hearing the Word of God, Adam's constant communion with God had him living the ultimate design as a man walking the earth but with a kingdom of God consciousness.

He partakes of every good thing earth has to offer with full access to the unlimited resources of the faith realm of the kingdom of heaven. It all falls apart when Adam and Eve become influenced by the word of Satan and put their faith in his words. They wind up becoming uncomfortable with operating in the kingdom of God because of sin and attempt to hide from His presence, and God becomes uncomfortable dealing with them and locks them out of the Garden of Eden. Man enters an age of struggle in hearing from God and becomes more comfortable with the earth realm and the culture of Satan. Satan's ideas become natural for man and those tendencies have become the nature of man to this day. Man's nature is soulish and sensual as his thoughts and lifestyle are dictated by what is broadcast and heard in the common discourse. Tremendous strides in worldwide communication through satellite TV have caused horizontal kingdoms across the globe to influence each other in dress, life choices, music and pursuit of money and possessions.

When we come to Christ and become citizens of the kingdom of God, it is not the easiest thing to make the adjustment to a new lifestyle, ideas, language, and currency. A few years ago, my wife and I drove to Toronto to attend the Billy Graham School of Evangelism. We had never been to Niagara Falls and as we lingered to enjoy the view, I had intended to fill up on gas before we entered Canada. I forgot to gas up and after driving toward Toronto, I noticed an Esso gas station. What is now called Exxon in the US used to be called Esso, so I felt very comfortable driving into the station. My feelings of ease quickly turned to panic as I realized the pumps were in liters and the money on the signs was not US dollars. All of a sudden there were people lined up for gas behind me and I was trying to rack my brain to convert liters to gallons and wonder how to pay with my money and how much gas it could buy. Total confusion and anxiety!

Last year we spent a few days in Paris and my wife got determined to buy a pair of shoes she spied in a store window. I was not enthusiastic, first of all because of the exchange rate of the dollar versus the euro. But that problem was nothing compared to what was about to take place. Pastor Muriel grabbed the shoe and as the clerk came over she asked for her size (good taste will not allow me to state the size here). A look of shock and panic came over the clerk and she blurted something in French and ran for the manager. Not only did she not speak English, the manager explained that they have a whole different system of numbering shoe sizes. Fortunately they did not have her size and we were able to run out of the store. The next day, we found a store with a little more understanding manager who rather than try to understand our English and use a shoe size translation chart, decided it was easier to get out a French shoe measuring device and find out what size Muriel wore in their system. By the time we got off the plane in London, we realized that Paris was a lot of fun, but it was really a somewhat traumatic experience.

We felt anxious in those countries because we did not know how to convert our words to theirs and their currencies and sizes to ours. In short, we were not proficient in doing business in those foreign kingdoms and in the same way, it will take some effort and practice to learn the rules and culture of the kingdom of God and to learn to convert assets and energy of the earthly realm into spiritual. We all know that the more time we spend in a new environment, the more we will be able to understand the language and culture and become more comfortable operating in it. II Corinthians 5:16-18 says that *"Therefore, from now on, we regard no one according to the flesh. Even though we have known Christ according to the flesh, yet now we know Him thus no longer. Therefore, if anyone is in Christ, he is a new creation; old things have passed away; behold, all things have become new. Now all things are of God..."*

You are What You Hear

If you are to learn how to become adept at the culture of the kingdom and proficient in converting earthly stuff to faith, you will have to develop a hunger for the presence of the Lord and the Word of God. Because the kingdom of God is a vertical or spiritual one, its culture is not primarily detected with human eyesight. The primary organ of spiritual connection is through the ear or through the faculty of hearing. Although He may periodically use the visual to get our attention, the vast majority of God's dealings with man are through the medium of the spoken word. Paul concludes in Romans 10:17 *"So then faith comes by hearing, and hearing by the word of God."* Again the Hebrew writer states in chapter 1:1-3, *"God, who at various times and in various ways spoke in times past to the fathers by the prophets, has in these last days spoken to us by His Son, whom He has appointed heir of all things, through whom He also made the worlds; who being the brightness of His glory and the express image of His person, and upholding all things by the word of His power."*

When God was mentoring Adam in the Garden, Adam was familiar with His voice and responds when God came looking for Him by saying, *"I heard your voice in the garden and I was afraid because I was naked." Genesis 3:10.* When God called Abram in Genesis 12, the scripture states that *"Now the Lord had said to Abram."* God attracted Moses attention with a burning bush, but once He got him to look, God spoke from out of the bush. In Exodus 20 where God gives the Ten Commandments even though He wrote them on the tablets, His primary means of communication then and for the future was through the spoken word. Exodus 20:1 reads, *"And God spoke all these words, saying:"* He goes on to recite the commandments to Moses and instructs him to speak these words to the people. They were not to make graven images or statues and as result, historically Israel is not noted for many of the fine arts such as sculpture and paintings. But they were instructed to diligently recite the Word of God and the great miracles that He had performed on their behalf and teach them daily to their children. In Deuteronomy 6:6 the scripture reads, *"And these words which I command you today shall be in your heart. You shall teach them diligently to your children, and shall talk of them when you sit in your house, when you walk by the way, when you lie down, and when you rise up."*

It is interesting that Jews are known for their mastery of language and grammar because of God's insistence on the primacy of the spoken and written Word.

Let me take a moment to consider the practical challenge of hearing the voice of the Lord using Moses and the children of Israel as an example. When God was going to give the commandments to the people, they all assembled at Mt. Sinai with some limits on how close the people could get. Many were eager to get as close as possible until they witnessed all the thunderings, the lightning flashes, the sound of the trumpet and the mountain smoking. Then the people started trembling and moved away and said to Moses in Exodus 20:19, *"You speak with us, and we will hear; but let not God speak with us, lest we die."* God's intention has always been for His people to be a kingdom of priests, all with direct access to Him at all times, but the masses of those who align themselves with Him are not always eager to seek His presence and His word.

Therefore, God has used the voice of the prophet and the foolishness of preaching to speak to vessels that were willing to set themselves apart to hear from Him and then convey His message to believers. It takes a great deal of faith to believe that mental impressions, inner impulses, daydreams, inner voices, strong intuitions, etc. are actually God speaking to you. It takes even more faith to have the courage to take action based on such impressions.

Consider the dilemma Moses faced when he heard the voice of God speaking from the burning bush. The normal reaction of any man to that situation would be that he was having a mental breakdown. No one wants to go home and tell his wife that God was talking to him today out of a bush that was on fire but was not consumed. And on top of that, God was asking him to return to Egypt where he had fled because of a murder charge and to go and setup a meeting with the princes of Israel and relate his weird encounter and ask for their support in arranging a meeting with Pharaoh where he would demand that he let them all just leave.

That's a lot of faith to believe you are actually hearing all this from God. Many a person has been placed in a straight jacket for much less. The average believer is not willing to take such chances on the strength of what he perceives as God talking to him.

Beginning the Transition to a Life of Faith

Therefore, the beginning stages of faith building and making the transition from operating in the earth realm to moving in the realm of the kingdom is to gather yourself together with other believers in the House of the Lord where an atmosphere of faith is set through praise, worship, testimonies, prayer, fellowship and the preached Word. There we are encouraged to build ourselves up through personal prayer and daily Bible reading and a regular dose of Christian music and fellowship with other believers of like precious faith. We learn to take our hard earned money and convert some of it to spiritual substance through tithes and offerings, and we learn to convert our energy and creativity to the kingdom as we learn to present our bodies as a living sacrifice unto God.

We begin to allow the Holy Spirit to unlock the mysteries that surround our purpose and calling and become bolder in following the leading of the Spirit for the use of our gifts and in our dealings with people and circumstances that life presents to us. Daily we become more accustomed to kingdom culture and benefits. You know you are growing in the faith when you start to feel like Job in chapter 23:11-12, *"My foot has held fast to His steps; I have kept His way and not turned aside. I have not departed from the commandment of His lips; I have treasured the words of His mouth more than my necessary food."*

The purpose of this book is to move you to the place where it makes rational sense to convert every available asset under your command to kingdom purpose because you understand that everything becomes exceedingly more valuable when placed under His control and for His purposes.

You must make the transition that the way to obtain the desires of your heart is to seek first the kingdom of God and His righteousness and that He will add all the things you have in mind. You must not only believe that He is, but that He is a rewarder of those who diligently seek Him. You must believe that He intends to do exceedingly, abundantly more for you than you can ask or even think, according to His mighty power and not your power, ability or resources.

When you believe like this, you feel more comfortable in the presence of the Lord and operating in the kingdom of God than you do in the world. You can reap all the benefits of this world that are consistent with your beliefs in God, and yet not be under the control of the world's system and culture.

You didn't get saved just to go to heaven. In fact Jesus prayed in John 17 that the Father not take you out of this world, but would keep you from the evil in it. He wants a kingdom of priests that will show forth and demonstrate to the rest of the world the great benefits of being associated with His Name. The goal is to be saved and comfortable and proud about it.

"For I am not ashamed of the gospel of Christ, for it is the power of God to salvation for everyone who believes, for the Jew first, and also for the Greek. For in it the righteousness of God is revealed from faith to faith; as it is written, The just shall live by faith." *Romans 1:16-17*

Chapter Six - Some Things to Think About

Because we must operate in our relationship with God in the earth as well as the spirit, we have to become comfortable with the language and customs of the Kingdom of Heaven, and with the voice of God. In the earth, we can be deceived by what we see and hear, so God is particularly interested in connecting with us through the Word.

God may not come to us in a burning bush. But for some of us, even if He did, we may try to find a way to avoid hearing what He is telling us to do. You must have the faith to listen and truly hear God and to position yourself on a regular basis in an atmosphere that encourages your faith to grow.

1. Are the environments that you spend time in every week pleasing to God? (your home, your car, your job, your encounters, your social time?)

2. How much time do you dedicate to praise, worship, prayer, fellowship or study — or to just waiting on the Lord?

3. Are you striving to increase your knowledge and understanding of the Word of God and to know the language and culture of the Kingdom of Heaven?

4. What "other voices" may be distracting you from hearing the voice of the Lord?

Chapter 7
Faith That Attracts Interest

"Simon, Simon! Indeed, Satan has asked for you, that he may sift you as wheat. But I have prayed for you, that your faith should not fail; and when you have returned to Me, strengthen your brethren." Luke 22:31-32

What we are today is a product of what has attracted our attention in the past. When we are attracted to something, someone, or some idea, we will invariably use our love, energy, creativity, contacts, time and money to get to or acquire that thing. My wife is fond of the saying that *"what we love to do, we will find time to do."*

President Bill Clinton and the Monica Lewinsky escapade is one of the more captivating examples of attraction and connection of our time. You will recall the footage showing her strategically planting herself at a public appearance of the President along his path wearing a provocative dress and leaning over to give him a kiss. It was obvious from the video that because of her attraction for him, she was checking his schedule, preparing herself and her spot in the receiving line to attract his attention and to stand out to him in a crowd. She then went on to arrange a White House internship, and maneuvered her way into being able to walk by his Oval Office to again attract his attention. She successfully used her energy, creativity, contacts, time and money to stalk and attain what she hoped for.

Faith involves an assessment of where I am, how I have invested my substance (my love, energy, creativity, contacts, time and money) to get where I am, and finally how I am going to invest my substance from this point to move my life toward the picture I have for my future. Where I am today is where I have placed my faith in the past. If you are in a bad marriage today, it is a result of placing your faith in another person. You invested your substance (your love, energy, creativity, contacts, time and money) in that person to attract them to you and to keep the relationship going. We often stay in bad situations longer than is prudent simply because we have invested so much in it. The worse outcome for a relationship is to find that the other person has been unfaithful or has abused our faith.

If you are in a bad financial situation today, often it is because you were attracted to and invested in something or some venture that was unwise or unprofitable. Sometimes it was an attraction for too many dresses, or cars, or gambling, or drugs, or fast money. I'm fond of Breyer's Ice Cream and it's amazing to me that when I try to kick the habit, I'm mysteriously attracted to Giant Supermarket only to discover my favorite ice cream on sale for ½ price.

It is uncanny that what we are attracted to is attracted to us. What we are interested in has interest in us. What we are projecting will attract what is interested in what we are projecting. I remember many years ago being summoned to Brooklyn, NY by Bishop Wilbert McKinley to consult on his church sound system. I took the Greyhound Bus and when I emerged from the terminal I was accosted by at least three prostitutes in the first block out of the door. I was sure they were prostitutes because their dress clearly projected their business and if I had any doubts, their solicitations quickly put those to rest. They had invested their substance and faith in the world's oldest profession, and the fact that they were working the streets that night projected that they hoped to continue to reap profit from the investment of their love, energy, creativity, contacts and money in their prostitution vision.

The only way they could stay in business is that there were men who would be attracted to what they were projecting and soliciting. Therefore, people who are attracted to prostitutes will no doubt find the areas they work and have such faith in those affairs that they will use their love of that and their energy and creativity to keep from getting caught, and spend their hard earned money to enjoy that which they are attracted to. As an aside, it is always challenging for us to try to get our Christian young people to be careful in following fashion trends that make them project something that they are not. If they are not prostitutes and drug dealers, then why should they dress like they are.

In this next stage of your journey, carefully assess where your faith has landed you and where you will invest your substance next because faith or substance attracts interest. If someone wins the lottery, they will have to get an attorney and go into hiding, because their newfound substance will attract thousands of people with investment schemes as well as long lost friends and relatives. People who are known to have wealth are constantly bombarded by people interested in helping them to utilize their money. People who have achieved fame as an athlete, entertainer or even as a criminal will have the media and groupies stalking them everywhere they go.

Your next step will attract interest whether it is a positive direction or negative. There are only two spiritual kingdoms, and each will respond to your next step of faith. Each kingdom is attracted to you. Each kingdom is drawing on your faith. If you direct your faith (your love, energy, creativity, contacts, time and money) towards crack cocaine, you will attract other crack heads and crack dealers. You'll discover a nice crack head girl friend and a nice crack house to fellowship with other addicted people. You can even be in church but if you direct your faith (your love, energy, creativity, contacts and money) towards a few church gossipers or troublemakers, you will find every one of them in the church mysteriously attracted to you. You need to be very clear about where your faith is taking you.

When I was in high school at Baltimore City College, I was trying to master playing the organ and singing at the same time. It was difficult for me to concentrate on both at the same time. I really admire people that can do both well. One day while practicing, my mother called down to tell me I was singing off key. She then suggested that I should join the Glee Club at school to improve my singing.

It just happened that the next day at school there was an announcement that the Glee Club was looking for members. A classmate of mine who I had known from junior high told me he was also interested, so we both went to the choir room after school.

As I looked around the room, I was somewhat dismayed to observe that the Glee Club teacher at our all male school was obviously gay, as were too many members of the choir for my tastes. I told my buddy that I wasn't going to stick around and he responded that he really wanted to sing, so he was going to join. This was around March and by the end of the school year my friend had clearly become one of the "fella's." Thinking back on him, it's possible he already had gay tendencies, but he was clearly attracted by what the members of the Glee Club projected. I saw another schoolmate of mine a few years later and he told me our classmate had moved to New York and dressed as a woman.

Faith is Designed to Attract Interest

Because faith is the currency of heaven, when it is invested it is designed to attract interest. When we place money in the bank, they agree to pay us interest on our money. Bank of America in June 2005 offers a half of 1 % on regular savings accounts, 2.05% interest on Money Market Accounts with $2,500 or even up to $2,500,000, and a whopping 3.75% on a 10-year CD. They will turn around and invest your money by charging 18% to 24% interest to people with their credit cards. Generally, the more you place with the bank, the more interest you can attract.

Faith works in a similar way. The more of your substance (your love, energy, creativity, contacts, time and money) you invest in the pursuit and purposes of the kingdom of God, the more interest you will attract from the Lord. If you are a large depositor at the bank, you will attract more of the resources of the bank, more personalized service and more privileges. The bank is more interested in you and you receive higher interest from the bank than the person who has little invested in it. These days if you don't have an account, they will even charge you to cash a check that is drawn on their bank.

God's standard for relationship with Him has always been an intense and demanding one for he declares in Deuteronomy 6:5 *"You shall love the Lord your God with all your heart, with all your soul, and with all your strength."* Jesus reiterates this in the New Testament while being tested by a Pharisee attorney in Matthew 22:36-40 *"Teacher, which is the great commandment in the law?" Jesus said to him, "'You shall love the Lord your God with all your heart, with all your soul, and with all your mind.' "This is the first and great commandment. "And the second is like it: You shall love your neighbor as yourself.' "On these two commandments hang all the Law and the Prophets."*

Since He created us, His desire is that we be willing to invest all our faith substance in His kingdom and purpose, because His plans make the best use of our potential and the gifts that He placed in us. We are called His "peculiar" or "special" treasure, meaning a valued investment that one takes particular interest in and takes pains to keep secure.

Several years ago I became intrigued as I couldn't really find a place where Jesus took up an offering at any of his public meetings, yet He managed to run a large road ministry with at least 12 additional full-time staff who He was responsible for feeding and housing. Then I noticed Luke 8:1-3

"Now it came to pass, afterward, that He went through every city and village, preaching and bringing the glad tidings if the kingdom of God. And the twelve were with Him, and certain women who had been healed of evil spirits and infirmities-Mary called Magdalene, out of whom had come seven demons, and Joanna the wife of Chuza, Herod's steward, and

Susanna, and many others who provided for Him from their substance."

What a testimony to leave on record that these women had such kingdom insight that they would be willing to invest their substance in the ministry of Jesus to such an extent that He would never even have to lift an offering and it was such a powerful witness that the Bible would give us their names.

Since our faith comes by hearing the Word of God, when it is deposited in people who receive it and understand it, the Word produces interest on what has been deposited. In order to hear the Word, one will have to invest their substance of love, energy, creativity, contacts, time, and money to position themselves to hear and understand. That's what these special women did. But Jesus teaches in the parable of the sower in Matthew 13:23 that *"But he who received seed on the good ground is he who hears the word and understands it, who indeed bears fruit and produces: some a hundredfold, some sixty, some thirty."* Bank of America's best rate may be 3.75%, but Jesus has promised that depending on your willingness to invest your substance to receive the Word, He will cause it to yield up to a one hundred-fold return to you. *I invite the mathematicians to start calculating!*

There is unlimited power and levels of vision in developing a love and adherence to God's Word for Jesus states in John 15:5 & 7 that *"I am the vine, you are the branches. He who abides in Me, and I in him, bears much fruit; for without Me you can do nothing...If you abide in Me, and My words abide in you, you will ask what you desire, and it shall be done for you."* People willing to invest their faith substance in the Word and the Kingdom of God attract a banker who feels that it is His good pleasure to give us the kingdom.

Regularly Investing In Your Future

As a young boy I was always impressed with my mother's diligence in setting a goal and persisting until it was accomplished. One of my favorites was observing her handling her Christmas Club Savings Account. If memory serves me correctly, she would save quarters and dimes regularly throughout the year in little books that would give her an expected sum for Christmas shopping. Although I have never had the discipline to save money over extended periods of time, I have always understood the important principle of regularly investing and saving in a disciplined way, but because I have been self-employed for a good deal of my adult life, I have preferred to invest in my businesses and develop equity in property and put everything at my disposal into the ministry.

Believe me this approach is not a justification for not saving, but in the 1996 book *The Millionaire Next Door: The Surprising Secrets of America's Wealthy (Simon & Schuster, 1998),* the authors state that two-thirds of the millionaires are self-employed, with 75 percent of them entrepreneurs, and the remainder professionals such as doctors and accountants. "The idea that most people inherit wealth is outdated. A lot is built through businesses. Business creation is the No. 1 driver of wealth in this country," says Zultowski.

When I first started my recording studio, the SBA sent an old Jewish SCORE (Service Core of Retired Executives) Consultant to see me and he made a statement that I never forgot. He said "Son, take care of the business, and eventually the business will take care of you." I have taken that philosophy both in my business and in the ministry. By faith, I believe that my business ventures and ministry to the Lord will fulfill that promise.

Indeed, today the vast majority of Americans have probably not done as well as we should in regularly saving. According to *Business Week Online*, "Our Hidden Savings", Jan 2005), property seems to be our American priority. In 2004, the household savings rate averaged a meager 0.8% of disposable income (the rate was 7% over the three previous decades). This 0.8% is the lowest level of national savings since the Great Depression.

There is great power in regular savings, particularly if you are smart enough to start in your early twenties. According to Great Plains Trust Company, by saving $2,000 a year for 41 years and earning a 10% tax deferred investment return, an individual can accumulate a retirement savings of $1,000,000. Think about it-the total savings required is $82,000 (41 years multiplied by $2,000 per year) and the investment earnings is $918,000.

Obviously, our biggest enemy in a strategy like this is our desire to have stuff immediately that distracts us from the long-term goal of becoming a millionaire. Distractions rob us of our ability to keep our minds focused on the Lord which carries with it the promise of being kept in perfect peace or wholeness, not lacking anything.

The believer accepts easily the notion that the Holy Spirit is in us to guide and counsel us and that if we were not so distracted with the cares of this world, His direction would bring us the prosperity we desire. God knew the level of distraction we would face, so from the beginning of the Bible in Genesis, God devised a system of offerings and Sabbath that was designed to cause man to regularly turn his attention to God and convert a portion of his substance to kingdom purpose.

The whole notion of tithes, offerings, and worship is designed to get us in a regular mode of *"laying up for yourselves treasures in heaven, where neither moth nor rust destroys and where thieves do not break in and steal." Matthew 6:20* The willingness to devote a portion of your faith substance (love, energy, creativity, contacts, time and money) to spiritual purposes usually begins after an individual has had a spiritual encounter that brings them face to face with the reality of the spirit realm.

For example, Jacob in Genesis 28:20-22 had a dream with a ladder reaching to heaven and angels ascending and descending and after he awoke from his sleep *"Then Jacob made a vow, saying "If God will be with me, and keep me in this way that I am going, and give me bread to eat and clothing to put on, so that I come back to my father's house in peace, then the Lord shall be my God, and this stone which I have set as a pillar shall be God's house, and of all that You give me I will surely give a tenth to you."*

After Zacchaeus the tax collector had Jesus over for dinner in Luke 19:8 the scripture records *"Then Zacchaeus stood and said to the Lord, "Look, Lord, I give half of my goods to the poor, and if I have taken anything from anyone by false accusation, I restore fourfold."*

A final example is recorded in Acts 4:31-35 *"And the multitude of them that believed were of one heart and of one soul: neither said any [of them] that ought of the things which he possessed was his own; but they had all things common. And with great power gave the apostles witness of the resurrection of the Lord Jesus: and great grace was upon them all Neither was there any among them that lacked: for as many as were possessors of lands or houses sold them, and brought the prices of the things that were sold, And laid [them] down at the apostles' feet: and distribution was made unto every man according as he had need."*

In each case a genuine encounter with the realm of the kingdom immediately causes people to be willing to invest their precious substance in the purposes of God.

If you sense a reluctance to give your substance to honor the Lord with the firstfruits of all your increase (tithes) and you find it painful to be liberal in giving offerings, it is probably a good idea to examine your relationship with the Lord. It is possible you have not really met Him or that your response to meeting Him was like the rich, young ruler who shook his head and walked away, because he was more in love with his possessions than the idea of becoming a follower of Jesus.

Regular, thoughtful giving of our tithes and offerings and being generous to those in need brings us the promise of Proverbs 3:9-10 and Malachi 3:10 which reads *"Bring ye all the tithes into the storehouse, that there may be meat in mine house, and prove me now herewith, saith the LORD of hosts, if I will not open you the windows of heaven, and pour you out a blessing, that [there shall] not [be room] enough [to receive it]. And I will rebuke the devourer for your sakes, and he shall not destroy the fruits of your ground; neither shall your vine cast her fruit before the time in the field, saith the LORD of hosts. And all nations shall call you blessed: for ye shall be a delightsome land, saith the LORD of hosts.*

Regular, thoughtful giving to the house of the Lord requires the use of your faith and its accompanying substance to believe that by giving your substance without any further control of it, that God will in turn justify your faith with open heaven blessings.

Our giving attracts the interest of God. It will also attract the interest of Satan, who will not want to see resources that he previously had access to diverted to the kingdom of God. In Luke 22:31 Jesus warns Peter that Satan is attracted to him by stating *"Simon, Simon! Indeed, Satan has asked for you, that he may sift you as wheat. But I have prayed for you, that your faith should not fail; and when you have returned to Me, strengthen your brethren."* Faith just attracts interest so be prepared to have your commitment tested by sometimes unusual financial challenges as soon as you make up your mind to follow through on becoming a spiritual giver.

Personal Relationship Banking

Many banks today have merged into huge conglomerates that provide the convenience of national branches and ATM's. The downside is it often becomes more difficult to maintain a personal relationship with people at the bank. It's a great comfort to get to know the employees and manager of the branch you frequent and many banks create advertising campaigns around the slogan of "personal relationship banking." In a lot of cases it is nothing more than a slogan because personnel changes so often in many banks that it is a challenge for a customer to keep up.

I often use the bank branch near my house and had developed a great relationship with everyone there, but last summer while we were doing summer camp, it was more convenient to use the branch near our church. After camp concluded, I rushed to the branch near my house with a contractor to get some cash for some work that his crew had shown up to do. When I ran towards the ATM, I discovered that I did not have my wallet, nor did I have my checkbook. To make matters worse, the gas tank was empty and I was going to buy gas after I went to the machine. No wallet, not enough gas to get back home and back, no checks, no identification! I was momentarily in an embarrassed panic, but I quickly remembered that I knew the people in the bank. I confidently strode into the bank only to go into further panic as I looked around for a teller or manager that I recognized. Unfortunately, on this Saturday morning I knew no one, but I decided to give it a shot anyway. As I waited my turn I approached the available teller and began to tell my no ID story and the teller interrupted me and said that she knew who I was and was familiar with our ministry and watched me on TV. I was able to get a blank check and cash it without any ID because she knew who I was.

Friend, the most awesome wonder of the universe is that the God that created everything and everybody personally designed you, has big plans for you, and is so intimately acquainted with you that He knows the number of hairs on your head. He knows everything about you and gives each of us the open invitation to develop as close and personal a relationship with Him as we desire. How He is able to do this is unfathomable to our minds, but that's what makes Him God.

Actually, the idea of an omnipresent God who can

interact with all of us at the same time is certainly becoming more and more understandable to the human mind and experience. Technological breakthroughs of modern society have made the concepts of God's omnipresence, omniscience, and omnipotence understandable to us all. I remember so clearly being in Sunday School when our teacher was introducing the idea of the "*omni's*" to us. My little brain was reeling with how in the world God could be in all places at the same time and know everything. It just seemed to be a bit much.

But today, we can all turn on our TV's in America and watch the same show or news or sporting event from the comfort of our family room. And not only in America, but the telecast can be viewed all over the world. Not only that, I can be in checkout line number 12 at Wal-Mart and in an instant the credit card reader can assess the state of my account and allow the transaction while simultaneously performing the same check for every person in each line in that store and in stores and ATM's, and from 800 numbers and internet shopping transactions all over the world. As a person with a computer programming background, I still marvel myself each time at how quickly the approval transaction takes place.

We are created in God's image and likeness and every day we learn to think and perform more like Him. The internet is so modeled after the mind of God that it astounds me. In the past when you were having a discussion and people were speculating about some fact, we would just argue our guess. Recently we saw Roberta Flack on TV and noted that she really looked good. We started wondering about her age and rather than continuing to guess we just typed in a question on "Google" and within seconds we were presented with not only her age but all kinds of websites with every thing one would want to know about her. And every day it becomes more powerful as a source of information.

The grand point is that in an increasingly merged and impersonal world, we still have the wonderful privilege of knowing our banker intimately. He knows about things that are laid up for us that we have no idea about, and He has made arrangements for us to have every tool and resource necessary to fulfill His perfect will for our lives and we just need to take the time to get to know Him and His ideas for us better. Our credit system may disqualify people for certain benefits, loans, grants, etc. because of past credit issues, but our banker is more concerned about our future than our past mistakes. God's credit repair system erases and expunges our record by the blood of His dear Son Jesus Christ, and Paul declares in II Corinthians 5:17 *"Therefore, if anyone is in Christ, he is a new creation; old things have passed away; behold, all things have become new."*

In your every day banking situation, you may have a good relationship with the tellers, or the manager, but few of us will normally have a close relationship with the CEO of the entire bank. But isn't it exciting to know that because of faith we can really have a personal relationship with the CEO of the Banking System of the Kingdom of God.

Chapter Seven - Some Things to Think About

The position that you are in today is a direct result of what you have placed your faith in the past. As we direct our faith to what we are attracted to, it becomes attracted to us. Just as investments in the natural realm attract more wealth, our faith currency attracts the interest of God.

Sometimes the investment we have made of our love, energy, creativity, contacts, time and money have carried us so far off course we don't have the heart to change. But we are the peculiar treasure to God and He desires to give you the Kingdom. All that is required is that we make a consistent, sincere, regular investment with God and we will see an attraction that is growing stronger day by day.

1. Are your pursuits and investments more attractive to the Kingdom of Heaven or of this World?

2. Would you be comfortable with God examining the things you are attracted to?

3. What would it take for you to increase the level of your giving to God?

4. Can you say today that you are a friend of God, and can God say that of you?

Chapter 8
Living By Faith

"The just shall live by faith." Romans 1:17

At the beginning of this book I described the conversation that God had with me in 1976 that He was going to teach me about faith and my wife's miraculous healing of the tumor. After the euphoria of the healing, God would begin a new phase of faith training. I was managing the main Public Office of the C&P Telephone Company at the time, but my real passion was Praise Recordings, a professional music recording studio that I had started with several friends in 1973 and devoted most evenings and weekends to building the business. We had started in a run-down building in downtown Baltimore as a 4 track operation and had now moved to a nicer building and God was blessing us to record many of the churches and Gospel groups in the Baltimore-Washington area. The state of the art studios were

16 and 24 track operations, but I was just trying to figure out how to raise about $10,000 to move up to an 8 track studio.

One day I was sitting in a Kentucky Fried Chicken restaurant on Howard Street and in walked Joe Bradley, the owner of a 16 track studio several blocks away who was my main competitor. He had been in the business for over 14 years and for years did the bulk of the Christian recording in our area. I had recorded there on numerous occasions with people like Bishop Alfred Reaves and other groups I played for. Ironically, I was reading a book by President Jimmy Carter entitled "Why Not the Best," when Bradley greeted me by saying that he had been trying to get in touch with me because he wanted to find out if I was interested in taking over his studio.

We met and began discussing my purchase of his business for $100,000. He asked me if I could come up with $10,000 and setup a meeting with a SCORE (Service Core of Retired Executives) consultant. I spent the entire weekend prior to the meeting racking my brain as to how to come up with the money. I thought about selling all our equipment, and then I thought about selling my wife and children (Ha!). My father and I went to the meeting and the gentleman asked how much money we had and my father replied "about $5,000." To our surprise, he said for us to hold onto it, but he was going to recommend that we receive an SBA loan for the full amount and we wouldn't need any of our own money. We walked out of the meeting in a Holy Ghost daze. I had spent the whole weekend in full blown anxiety over raising $10,000 and God had already arranged the purchase without my help.

I marveled at how God had guided me into that restaurant on that particular day, at that particular time, and how he had arranged for Bradley to come to that same place at the same time. We had not seen each other in over 4 years. I marveled at the way I worried and God simply arranged things that I certainly had no control over. I marveled at how my aspiration was so small compared to what God had in mind for me at that point in my life.

It was surreal that one day my most expensive microphone was $200 and the next day I had a variety of $2,000 microphones at my disposal. One day I had a $200 reverb unit and the next day I had an $8,000 reverb system. One day I had a $1,000 hand made control console and the next day I had a $25,000 console. One day I had a $1,400 4 track recorder and the next day I had a $20,000 16 track recorder. Not only did I begin to experience the reality of *"the steps of a good man are ordered by the Lord,"* but I also began to understand the reality that God *"is able to do exceedingly, abundantly above all that we ask or think, according to the power that works in us." Ephesians 3:20.*

I could write a book about the faith lessons from Praise Recordings (and I probably will), but I want to point out the importance of the principle that the Apostle James stresses in James chapter 2:17 where he writes *"Thus also faith by itself, if it does not have works, is dead."*

Faith is the currency of heaven and it is designed to move or circulate. If you have $20,000 under your mattress for 10 years, you may have a feeling of financial security, but as long as it is under the mattress it does or accomplishes nothing. **Ideas, visions, opportunities, and open doors mean little if there is no corresponding action to bring them to meaningful reality.**

In Matthew 25:26 Jesus gives a parable of the talents and chastises the servant who buried the talent he had been given for investment by saying to him, *"... You wicked and lazy servant, you knew that I reap where I have not sown, and gather where I have not scattered seed. So you ought to have deposited my money with the bankers, and at my coming I would have received back my own with interest."* The Lord is not happy about people who do nothing with what He has invested in us.

After we met with the SCORE consultant, I had to go to the SBA (Small Business Administration) and begin the application process. The stack of forms was several inches thick and I had to put a package together that took me weeks to fill out. This was the mid 1970's so banks were not very accommodating to doing business loans for African-Americans, but the program still required me to be turned down first by two banks before I could get a direct loan from the SBA.

I was referred to several of the most conservative banks in town. It was really a lot of fun to go in and explain that I was purchasing a business with the help of the SBA and before I could finish the spiel the banker would say "Oh, you're here to get a turn down letter?" And they would proceed to gleefully whip one out for me. This type of experience would normally be humiliating, but it wasn't because I knew that it was just part of the process.

Be Willing to Do The Qualifying Work

After I attended the loan closing and settled into my new studio, I realized that the whole process and the stack of paperwork was simply a qualifying test. It was almost as if the SBA had created a process that if an applicant had the tenacity to fill out the papers and go through even the humiliating steps, you were automatically approved. I began to realize that countless people had probably been so intimidated by the stack of forms and the exhaustive nature of the process that many quit before they even started.

Is it possible that you have invested your faith substance in the kingdom and God has opened the windows of heaven for you and given you vision and purpose and you have been intimidated by the amount of work that will be required? To move through the doors God opens for you will take all of your love, energy, creativity, contacts, time and money both to get it up and to keep it running. The doors God opens are not entered by slackers!

When God gave Noah the opportunity to save his family and all the living species it came with over a hundred years of **WORK**. When God created Adam and placed him in a paradise-like estate he *"put him in the garden of Eden to tend it and keep it." Genesis 2:15*. He put him there to work. God will fight your enemies, but you have to have the courage to show up and get in the game.

The Courage to Make the Transition To Living By Faith

I was now 26 years old and had been married for seven years and had a wife and three small children and a mortgage. I had a good job with benefits. But now I had the business I had dreamed of which would demand my full time attention. I was excited about leaving the telephone company to pursue my dream and I wanted my wife to continue to stay at home and care for the children. Up to that time I had my personal checkbook and one for the part-time Praise Recordings. Two streams of income that could supplement each other if necessary.

My first week after leaving the telephone company, I came to the startling fact that the only stream I had would be coming from the Praise Recordings checkbook. I had no established contracts and no guaranteed business. For the first time in my life, I felt as though I was out on a faith limb. Lord, if business does not come through those doors, we will not be able to eat or pay the mortgage.

I was now knee deep in HGU (Holy Ghost University) semester number two. It was a crazy time to wake up many mornings realizing that I would need $2,000 or $3,000 that day and have no idea where it would be coming from when I left home. **These things will greatly impact your prayer life**. I began to learn what Paul had in mind in I Thessalonians 5:16-18 *"rejoice always, pray without ceasing, in everything give thanks; for this is the will of God in Christ Jesus for you."*

Nearly thirty years later there is hardly a half hour that passes in the day that I am not engaged in prayer. I may be having a conversation with you, but believe me, I'm praying while I'm talking, I'm praying while I'm preaching, I'm praying while I'm driving, I'm praying without ceasing because I've never been allowed to climb off that faith limb.

At some point in your faith walk, you will have to step out of the boat and attempt to walk out on the water toward what appears to be Jesus calling you to come where He is. Walking on water is simply you moving into a place where you are pretty sure that what He is asking you to do is way beyond your control. You realize the danger of sinking and you may sink from time to time, but the powerful lesson is that the Lord is always there to catch you and lift you up where He intended you to be. It is the reality of His assurance that He will never leave you or forsake you.

It will be a tragedy if you never have the courage to pursue the calling that is on your life and invest your substance in the vision that God has given you. God smeared purpose in you and your joy and fulfillment is tied to your willingness to take faith action to bring your kingdom purpose down into this realm. The anointing that is in you can only be activated by your action. Paul said in Philippians 3:12 *"...but I press on, that I may lay hold of that for which Christ Jesus has also laid hold of me."*

Investing all your eggs in Jesus' basket is not without a fight to maintain the peace of God which surpasses understanding, and anyone who knows me can see in my gray hairs that I have the evidence of fighting the good fight of faith. However, I feel like these gray hairs are like the limp that Jacob walked with after He wrestled with God: a gentle reminder that the only way to reign as a prince with God is to be reminded that God is the Boss and my blessings come from Him.

In those studio days, God arranged a line of business for me to record most of the Full Gospel Businessmen and Women's Aglow meetings in the Baltimore area. I would record the meetings and have cassette tapes available afterward. It was a great faith builder to go out several nights a week and hear great testimonies from businessmen and women and wonderful preachers. I will never forget hearing Pastor Jack Hayford for the first time at a Regional Full Gospel Businessmen's Convention in Washington preach a message called "Gambling With God." He talked about God's use of the "lot" to make His will known to men in the Bible and suggested that we be willing to take a gamble on God. That's my message to you. If you are going to take a risk on anything and with anybody, surely God is a good bet. The kingdom operates solely on faith and if you are saved and part of the kingdom, you won't really enjoy the benefits of the kingdom until you begin to live by faith.

Chapter Eight - Some Things to Think About

Faith is the currency of God and it is designed to circulate. For many of us the talents the Lord has given us stay buried in our minds, in our heart, in a file folder, or in our dreams and never become manifested because we cannot take what the world calls a leap of faith.

Part of the exercise of your faith is the willingness to put aside any doubts, insecurity or fears and put your faith into action! In every level there are going to be steps you must take to get access to the things you need to have success. We should not be discouraged by the stops and starts, but consider them part of the process of qualifying for the promises of God.

Faith— Access Card To The Kingdom of Heaven

The Bible says faith without works is dead

1. Would others say you are a worker and a giver or only a receiver?

2. Are you taking faith steps every day to seize the opportunities that God is presenting you, or are you running in the other direction to avoid responsibility?

3. How much faith have you put in a vision or purpose God has given you in the last year, month, week, day?

4. Is the most humiliating experience you can imagine worth the joy of fulfilling your kingdom purpose?

Chapter 9
The Trial of Your Faith

"That the trial of your faith, being much more precious than of gold that perisheth, though it be tried with fire, might be found unto praise and honour and glory at the appearing of Jesus Christ." I Peter 1:7

We all know that our potential in Christ is vast and that we must unleash our faith to move to the next level in our purpose. In order to picture where we are going, we have talked about our ongoing assessment of where we are and where the investment of our faith substance (love, energy, creativity, contacts, time and money) has been invested in the past.

The truth is that you have probably been motivated by past hopes and dreams that you are convinced were divinely inspired. You may have gone to a business presentation and become so excited that you had trouble sleeping for days, or maybe you have had a life long desire to accomplish some goal and have expended tons of resources to that end. You have probably tortured yourself with wondering is this God, my own ambition, or even the devil that is leading me to pursue this objective. This is the exciting and yet daunting challenge of spiritual discernment. It would be so much easier if God would just send us an official email or certified letter.

As a result we find ourselves seeking Him in prayer and meditation and reading His Word. We go to church hoping that something is said that will validate our direction. Maybe some prophet will miraculously call us out in a service and confirm exactly what we are doing. I'm fond of saying that God automatically enrolls all of us in HGU (Holy Ghost University) and He designs the curriculum, the quizzes, the final exams, and our graduations. He is determined to teach us how to listen to the still, small voice within to have faith that our steps are ordered by Him.

The tricky part is that we just don't know the schedule and not knowing the schedule is the central ingredient in the trial of our faith. If you were to go to the bank tomorrow with $20,000 to invest in a savings program, you could look at the bank's options and get a clear picture of the interest rates for various instruments along with the date it would mature. If you invest your substance in a 36 month CD at 2% interest, you could get a calculation of the final reward and know precisely when you could cash it in. The intervening 36 months becomes a trial of your faith in this investment. Will you have the fortitude to leave the investment in the bank despite the challenges of day to day living. Surely, the car will break down, or the furnace, or the roof will spring a leak, or you'll become exhausted and desperately require a cruise.

Secondly, if you invest the $20,000 in the 36 month CD, you probably won't go back to the bank next week excitedly inquiring about how much your investment is now worth or expecting that it has matured in one week. Sadly, I have seen many a person come to the Lord and begin attending church and Bible Class and giving their tithes and offerings and excitedly expecting that after two months their marriage will be fixed, bankruptcy reversed, they will have been promoted on the job, and have launched their new ministry. Some will sadly conclude that it doesn't work and that it is a waste of substance and they will return to investing in the manner they have been accustomed in the past. But no rational person would determine that the bank was a failure because a 36 month CD had not come to maturity in 2 months.

After spending over 36 months with Jesus, the disciples asked Him in Acts 1:6-7 *"Therefore, when they had come together, they asked Him, saying, "Lord, will You at this time restore the kingdom to Israel?" And He said to them, "It is not for you to know times or seasons which the Father has put in His own authority. "But you shall receive power when the Holy Spirit has come upon you."* They felt pretty sure that they had put in enough time to cash in, but Jesus let them know that they would not be given the schedule, but they would be given power and authority to fulfill their part in bringing the kingdom to pass.

It is as if you are approaching the Bank of the Kingdom of Heaven and you encounter the Investment Choices Sign something like this:

The Bank of The Kingdom Of God		
Investment Amount	**Interest Rate**	**Maturity Time**
All Substance Amounts Accepted – No Minimum – We Advise 10% of Your Gross Income – For Best Results Bring Everything You Have	No Fixed Rate – We Specialize in Adjustable Interest Rates Dependent on What You Will Need To Carry Out Your Purpose	At the Sole Discretion of Bank Management. The Fully Matured Value Could Be Made Available To You at Anytime from Immediately to Years from Now. We Know Exactly When the Proper Time Will Be – Have Faith
There is A Penalty For Early Withdrawal		

God gave Abraham such great promises concerning the vastness of his descendants when he and his wife were childless. They kept waiting for the promise to come, and no doubt they worked hard at their end to get Sarah pregnant, but nothing happened and they started getting real old. Sarah gets so far beyond child bearing that they have taken matters into their own hands with Hagar and Ishmael and have just given up on having a son. This becomes another in a long series of trials of Abraham's faith. It is no longer just when, but also how. That may be a very real concern for you today also. We also may jump to conclusions that we misunderstood God's promise to us and step in ourselves to help Him out. We may have grown as cynical as Sarah who laughed at the promise but I believe the Lord may be saying to us just as He said to her *"Is anything too hard for the Lord? At the appointed time I will return to you.." Genesis 18:14*

There is an appointed time when the Lord will return to you all the substance you have invested, but when it comes back to you Jesus promised that it would be *"given to you: good measure, pressed down, shaken together, and running over will be put into your bosom." Luke 6:38* The trial of your faith is a test of your being able to trust God with the interest rate and the matured release of the blessing.

Penalties For Early Withdrawal

Every bank investment sign carries a warning about

penalties that will be assessed for withdrawing your investment before the maturity date. When you invest your substance with the bank for a stipulated period, they know they have the use of those funds to loan out and to use at their discretion for that period. If people started coming in and taking their money out at any time, the bank would have chaos. So to discourage that practice and help people get their investment to maturity, the bank imposes monetary penalties for early withdrawal. You have to compensate the bank to get to your own investment because after you invested it, it really became the bank's money for the period.

In a similar manner, when we invest our faith substance in the kingdom, we release it into the care and direction of the Lord who causes our investment of love, energy, creativity, contacts, time and money to bring about harvest in the lives of others and in kingdom ministry. Unlike our investment in a CD where we put money in and expect money with money interest back, in the kingdom we may get back our investment in ways that we were not expecting.

Paul says in Romans 8:26-28 that *"Likewise the Spirit also helps in our weaknesses. For we do not know what we should pray for as we ought, but the Spirit Himself makes intercession for us with groanings which cannot be uttered. Now He who searches the hearts knows what the mind of the Spirit is, because He makes intercession for the saints according to the will of God. And we know that all things work together for good to those who love God, to those who are the called according to His purpose."* Beloved, we have a banker that has more clarity about what to do with our investment and how to return it to us than we do, so we can relax and rejoice in the fact that all things are working together for our good. You may be praying for a raise, and God may be arranging a whole new career!

Bishop Don Meares of Evangel Church in Maryland shared a great insight regarding the windows of heaven that Malachi prophesied would open to those who are faithful in giving tithes and offerings. He stated that there are two main purposes for windows. First, they allow us to see the heavens from what would be a closed environment, and secondly, they allow the light from the heavens to enter into a room that would be dependent on artificial light. Thus the windows of heaven that are opened to us allow us to see out of our limited environment into the heavenly realm and also to receive kingdom revelation instead of human ideas. When you are facing difficult situations, we need open windows within to see God's way of escape and find victory solutions for our lives.

In Genesis 26 Isaac was facing a famine situation and began to direct his thoughts to solving the problem in the way that his father Abraham did in his early walk with God. He determined that the way out of the famine was to go down to Egypt, but God stopped him and admonished him to stay in the land of promise and reiterated to him all the promises of prosperity that were given for his family. Despite the trial of his faith that the famine presented the Bible says that *"Then Isaac sowed in that land, and reaped in the same year a hundredfold; and the LORD blessed him. The man began to prosper, and continued prospering until he became very prosperous; for he had possessions of flocks and possessions of herds and a great number of servants." Genesis 26:12-14.* He sowed his substance in the midst of famine conditions and received blessings in all sorts of wonderful forms. But there was the trial period of one year in a famine and not having any idea when the trial would be over.

Trials of Famine, Wilderness, & Fear

When you respond by faith to the picture God has shown you for your next assignment, there is always the euphoria of the moment. Abram barely got into the Promised Land when he realized he was smack in the middle of a famine. It's amazing that you can get right in the will of God and right in the midst of the celebration, and then find yourself having difficulty.

You'll remember the dancing and singing of the children of Israel as Pharaoh's army drowned in the Red Sea and they knew that they were finally free from their enslavement. The singing had barely died down when they traveled three days into the wilderness looking for water and when they finally found some they discovered it was undrinkable. When they realized the Promised Land was nearby and sent spies out to examine it, they became filled with fear because the inhabitants of the land were giants.

Our arrival at our faith destination qualifies us for the test that will challenge the focus of our faith after we arrive. I remember a member at our church who was praying for a customized conversion van. After he got it, he excitedly told us he wouldn't be able to come to church the next few weeks because he would be hitting the road on the weekends to break in his new van. He's still missing in action years later.

I'm reminded of Deuteronomy 8 where the scripture reads *"¹Every commandment which I command you today you must be careful to observe, that you may live and multiply, and go in and possess the land of which the LORD swore to your fathers. ²And you shall remember that the LORD your God led you all the way these forty years in the wilderness, to humble you and test you, to know what was in your heart, whether you would keep His commandments or not.."* And further *"¹⁰When you have eaten and are full, then you shall bless the LORD your God for the good land which He has given you. ¹¹"Beware that you do not forget the LORD your God by not keeping His commandments, His judgments, and His statutes which I command you today."*

In the inevitable period of famine, wilderness, or fear that comes to test where you will invest your faith, become more diligent in seeking His face, more committed to walking upright before Him, and more determined to keep making Him the object of your faith. Don't get confused and *"...say in your heart, "My power and the might of my hand have gained me this wealth.' ¹⁸"And you shall remember the LORD your God, for it is He who gives you power to get wealth, that He may establish His covenant which He swore to your fathers, as it is this day."*

Trials of Our Faith – The Gateway to Your Next Level

The apostle James writes in chapter 1 *"My brethren, count it all joy when you fall into various trials, knowing that the testing of your faith produces patience. But let patience have its perfect work, that you may be perfect and complete, lacking nothing." James 1:2-4* When we invest in the bank CD, we have to patiently wait for it to mature before using it or reinvesting it. James encourages us that the trials that test our faith investments produce a patience and confidence in us that not only matures our investment, but matures us in the faith. At the end of the trial we are found to have grown and become complete, lacking nothing.

I remember when graduation time was approaching from college. I was so busy trying to study for tests, and write papers that I became anxious one day to double check that I had met all the graduation requirements. You had to have a certain number of credits to graduate and you had to have the right mix of credits for the particular degree. I realized that I hadn't paid much attention to all this in quite some time. What a relief it was to go to the office and verify that I had met all the requirements for graduation and I would be moving on to the next phase of my life.

I think back on taking tests throughout school and like most people, I generally was not excited about them. The studying, the anxiety, and the waiting for results was not an enjoyable process. In high school, I began to take another approach when it came time for the PSAT, SAT, National Merit Scholarship Qualifying Test, and various aptitude tests. I actually began to look forward to these with a degree of anticipation because it was clear that these tests were **gateways** to the next level. They became exciting challenges and opportunities to get an idea of where you stood with others nationally and the results could create interest from colleges.
I did fairly well on the PSAT and National Merit tests and the response I found in the mail each day from colleges that I had never even heard of was unbelievable. I had taken a test at Baltimore City College on a Saturday and for months after the test all these colleges were interested in investing in me.

When I went to college, the pressure and the competition was intense and testing was again a source of anxiety for the first few years. I started out in Operations Research and Industrial Engineering and when I received my acceptance information I had to go do some research to find out what in the world Operations Research was. Test taking the first few years was not pleasant.

Later I adjusted my major to Business & Industrial Management as I began to understand where my gifts and aptitude lay. Now I was writing papers about things I was passionate about. Now studying became an adventure. Needless to say, my grades soared and I felt I was now at the head and not the tail. Tests again became an opportunity to express and formulate my views. The Graduate Record Exam became another gateway for graduate school and an opportunity to go to the next level.

It's apparent that there is a major difference in how we view testing when we are operating in our purpose and feel that we have had adequate preparation for the test and that the test is just our validating experience to show that we are ready for elevation. The trial of your faith is a HGU requirement specifically designed for your specially designed curriculum and is simply a validation experience to complete this level.

James 1:2 says that we should *"Count it all joy when you fall into various trials."* Take the time to really study your Bible and thoroughly equip yourself for the pop quizzes and exams that are coming your way. Jesus has assured us that *"These things I have spoken to you, that in Me you may have peace. In the world you will have tribulation; but be of good cheer, I have overcome the world." John 16:32-34* Joy, good cheer and trial and tribulation seem like strange bed-fellows, but if you know that you have a CD maturing at the bank, generally it does not cause anxiety except when you are tempted to cash it in because you are experiencing a financial crisis. If you are able to make it through the immediate crisis with your investment intact, it becomes a source of joy and pride. God wants you to go through and endure your trials and tests for the *"joy that is set before you." Hebrews 12:2.*

Keep your eyes on Jesus as He brings you to full maturity through your trials and *"do not cast away your confidence, which has great reward, For you have need of endurance, so that after you have done the will of God, you may receive the promise." Hebrews 10:35*

Chapter Nine - Some Things to Think About

The testing of our faith is the gateway to getting to the next level. Not knowing the schedule of God is the central ingredient in the trial of our faith. Often times the greater the return, the longer will be the trial. As we grow weary of waiting we can often suffer the penalties of early withdrawal: famine, the wilderness, and fear.

But God operates in appointed times. We must believe that He has ordained the exact time when all the substance that you have invested will yield its increase. Once you have been qualified by the

Faith— Access Card To The Kingdom of Heaven

test, you will find that His idea of a return goes far beyond what you can ask or think.

1. Are you placing faith in your or another's history with God or trusting God's timing for your current situation?

2. Take a moment to assess: Is there yet more I need to invest of my love, energy, creativity, contacts, time and money for the Kingdom of God?

3. In my current trial of faith, am I prepared or have I short-changed God and how can I redeem it back?

4. If you are facing a particular test, can you still see Jesus and the vision He has for you?

Chapter 10
Where is Your Faith

"But He said to them, "Where is your faith?" And they were afraid, and marveled, saying to one another, "Who can this be? For He commands even the winds and water, and they obey Him!"
Luke 8:25

You have faith whether you are consciously investing it or not. Your faith substance consists primarily of your love, energy, creativity, contacts, time and money, and you are currently investing these priceless assets that are under your control. What are you passionate about at this stage of your life? If you were to look at your schedule for the past week, where did you spend the bulk of your time when you were not at work or asleep?

At our couple's retreats I often do an exercise where

I ask each spouse to assume that they just received an unexpected $50,000 windfall. They are asked to write out how they would spend or invest the windfall and then they come together to compare their choices with their mate. It reveals a lot about where their heart is, their vision is, and where their faith is.

How much of your substance are you investing in seeking God's divine purpose for your life and your family or are you consumed with the pursuit of stuff? Often we are spending our lives attempting to provide a safety net against the storms of life.

In the passage at the beginning of this chapter Jesus and his disciples are on a boat cruise that He has arranged. He mapped out a destination and said *"Let us cross over to the other side of the lake."* *Luke 8:22* Jesus decides to take a nap and a terrible storm arrives, the boat starts taking on water and these experienced fisherman conclude that they are in jeopardy of going under. After Jesus awakens and tells the storm to shut up, He turns to them and asks *"Where is your faith."*

It seems to me they had about three or four choices. Their faith could be in their marine experience when dealing with previous storms and that amount of water in the boat. Or, their faith could be in the ring leader who at some point declared they were in jeopardy and we need to wake Jesus, or their faith could be in the power of the storm, or, finally their faith could be in the Word of Jesus who said they were going to the other side of the lake. It's probably unrealistic for most of us, but I feel like the real faith step would have been for Peter to stand up and say "Let's do what Jesus is doing – Let's all take a nap!" Let us pray that we would develop the mindset that our mission is to be doing what He is doing and saying what His Word is saying and investing in what He is interested in us investing our substance in.

In my first tour of duty with the telephone company (I had three), I worked there for a paycheck and benefits. I put my time in and put in the energy to ensure that my group would have top results. However, my love, my creativity, and my contacts were reserved for my budding recording studio business. It was the object of my passion and all my available time outside of church.

After five years I was able to leave the telephone company with my SBA loan and go full-time in the studio. After several years of not making enough money to satisfy the demands of a growing family and the pressure of living by faith, I ran into my old telephone company boss and he begged me to come back and help them. I thought I would be able to take a break from the pressure cooker and would be able to return to my passionless paycheck and benefits. It turned out to be an intense experience as I found myself now assigned to people that had interesting views of racial issues. You get my drift! Even worse was it was no longer a 9-5 workday as these folks would come in and work from 7 AM – 7 PM. Some break.

During this time I developed an avid interest in the emerging personal computer industry and began studying it on my own. I attended a Black Manager's Workshop at the telephone company which had a profound effect on my career and understanding of the investment of our substance. Essentially, the seminar leader challenged us to not think that we deserved promotion because of our resume, or because of our talent, but because of the passion and creativity we could bring to fashion solutions to problems that would set your work apart from others regardless of their race.

I realized that week that as creative as the Lord had blessed me to be, I had never used one ounce of creativity to enhance the telephone company operations. During that week, the Holy Spirit flooded me with ways that the personal computer could be used in the telephone company operations and I set about designing these systems even before I left that seminar that week.

I began devising these systems on my own time in the evenings and weekends without really telling anyone. Then the most amazing thing happened. My "red-neck" boss asked to take me to lunch which was very unusual. At lunch he mumbled that the Vice-President of C&P in Washington had expressed an interest in having me work for him to introduce personal computing into the telephone company. However, my boss kept telling him that he was sure I was not interested. They finally forced him to discuss it with me and of course I told him that I would take the train even to New York each day if I could escape from him!

I didn't get the original job, but soon after I became one of two PC Consultants with the responsibility to bring PC Technology and Training into the four C&P areas of Maryland, DC, Virginia and West Virginia.

It was as if the moment I was willing to invest some of my substance: my love, energy, creativity, contacts, time and money into the telephone company that unbelievable opportunities began to open for me. God gave me insight to do things and devise systems that even astounded me. Friend, I am convinced that if more people understood this principle of investing your substance in your job, your relationships, and particularly in your church and in the things of God, you will literally understand the windows of heaven opening for you.

I close this book with a brief lesson from John chapter 21 where the disciples are still reeling with how they are to function after the resurrection without Jesus' personal leadership on a daily basis. The events leading up to Jesus' arrest, crucifixion, resurrection and the way He just kept popping up had left them anxious and perplexed.

When we are under pressure, we often revert to what is comfortable from our past. Peter declares to the other disciples that he was going fishing, or going back to what he knew best. The others joined in and they toiled all night and caught nothing, just as they had when they first met Jesus. The story goes on to say that Jesus began giving them instructions from the shore about where to invest their energy to get some fish and after they saw the result they realized that it was Jesus.

After they had breakfast in verse 15 it reads *"When they had finished eating, Jesus said to Simon Peter, "Simon son of John, do you truly love me more than these?" "Yes, Lord," he said, "you know that I love you." Jesus said, "Feed my lambs."* Jesus began to challenge them about where their faith was invested by asking them to analyze what would be the object of their love. Would it be the fishing profession or ministry to the sheep of His pasture. To drive the point home he repeated the challenge two more times.

"What you love to do, You will find time to do." Where you invest your love, energy, creativity, contacts, time and money is your clearest indication of what and where you have your faith deposited. Make the wise choice to invest your substance in the advancement of God's purposes for it is there that your faith gives you 24-7 access to the unlimited resources of the Banking System of the Kingdom of God.

Chapter Ten - Some Things to Think About

In the end, the choice of where we place our faith and our substance in life is ours alone. We live out our faith in the midst of storms and in the company of others working out their own faith. We could get so close to Jesus and still have more trust in ourselves, or in the storm or in another ringleader.

We must stay passionate about keeping our faith in Jesus. God has designed it so that where we direct our passions will yield some increase. As we have been on this journey to increase our faith it is important to reach for all that God has for you. Do not be satisfied with anything less than what Jesus has planned for you.

1. Have you conquered the things that separate you from faith in Jesus?

2. Have you fully deposited your substance with God: your love, your energy, your creativity, your time, your contacts, your money?

3. Will you place your faith in Jesus to convert your investment to feed you and countless others to fulfill the purposes of God?

Printed in the United States
219508BV00001B/2/A